Designing Suburban Futures

New Models from Build a Better Burb

June Williamson

ISLANDPRESS

Washington | Covelo | London

Designing Suburban Futures:

New Models from Build a Better Burb

Island Press is a trademark of The Center for Resource Economics.

Library of Congress Cataloging-in-Publication Data

Williamson, June.
    Designing suburban futures : new models from build
a better burb / June Williamson.
      pages cm
      Includes bibliographical references and index.
      ISBN 978-1-61091-197-9 (cloth : alk. paper) –
      ISBN 1-61091-197-0 (cloth : alk. paper) –
      ISBN 978-1-59726-241-5 (pbk. : alk. paper) –
      ISBN 1-59726-241-2 (pbk. : alk. paper)
      1. Suburbs – United States – Planning.
      2. Sustainable development – United States. I. Title.
HT352.U6W55 2013
307.740973 – dc23   2013004177

British Cataloguing-in-Publication data available.

Printed on recycled, acid-free paper

Design: Thumb, New York
Type: Berthold Akzidenz Grotesk, Courier Sans

Manufactured in the United States of America

10 9 8 7 6 5 4 3 2 1

Keywords: Bourgeois utopias, Broadacre City, design competition, edge and edgeless cities, Great Recession, Long Island region, infill development, neighborhood design, redevelopment, regreening, re-inhabitation, retrofitting suburbia, suburban sprawl, suburbanization, urban-suburban reciprocity, urban resiliency

Designing_____

_____Suburban
_____Futures

For my father.

Contents

Vision: A Role for Design in Suburban Resilience

Exemplar: Building a Better Burb on Long Island

Preface

My call to action in this book, to design better suburban futures, is not a novel one. Many have preceded me, and others will follow. However, I do hope to have articulated and framed arguments and opportunities in a way that is clear and compelling, by bringing together several strands of research and design propositions, including the vivid examples from the 2010 Build a Better Burb ideas competition for the suburbs of Long Island, richly documented in these pages.

The history of suburbanization is long and complex, only skimmed in the overview chapter "Context for Change." The majority of North Americans — not just those in the middle classes — have spent decades building and living in predominantly suburban landscapes, and we must spend the next generation retrofitting these places for the new needs of the twenty-first century and beyond, to build a resilient future suburbia that is climate sensitive, with compact nodes of human settlement, pedestrian and bike friendly for better health, and responsive to changing demographics and contemporary sustainable lifestyles. While designers, critics, and theorists have been probing, questioning, and re-envisioning the suburban environment we built for ourselves for some time, the urgency to halt sprawl and transform the most unsustainable and nonresilient aspects of suburbs has increased significantly. The time to act is *now*.

Generous support for this publication was provided by an Individual Project Award, sponsored by the Van Alen Institute, from the New York State Council on the Arts with the support of Governor Andrew Cuomo and the New York State Legislature, an Individual Grant from the Graham Foundation for Advanced Studies in the Fine Arts, and a PSC-CUNY Award, jointly funded by the Professional Staff Congress and the City University of New York. I offer sincere thanks to these organizations and their staff.

I also want to thank Nancy Rauch Douzinas and the Rauch Foundation for taking initiative to sponsor the Build a Better Burb competition from within the Long Island Index Project and for inviting me to consult. It was a tremendously valuable opportunity. I commend the staff, especially Long Island Index project director Ann Golob, for ongoing dedication to disseminating ideas generated through the competition with an exemplary website. I salute their willingness to engage the power of thoughtful, creative design, generated from good information, to effect needed change.

I extend heartfelt thanks to Ellen Dunham-Jones for her intellectual partnership over many years, and also to the cadre of urban design peers who formed the jury for the competition and contributed their intellectual and creative energy to evaluating hundreds of submissions. Kudos and best wishes to my capable assistants, former students all: Thomas Faust and Timothy Miron for the book, Marielly Casanova and Kelly Greenfield for the competition. My editor at Island Press, Heather Boyer, was a consummate pro, and my graphic designer, Luke Bulman of Thumb, was a godsend, for both the overall book design and infographics. I must also bow down to all the talented designers who were sufficiently intrigued to enter the competition, to tackle the challenge of redesigning suburbia, with verve, nerve, enthusiasm, wit, chutzpah, and vision, and to explore and share their bold ideas.

Lastly, I extend my sincerest gratitude to my husband, David Schiminovich, and son, Theo, for their unwavering support and good cheer. With deepest love, I dedicate this book to my dear father, John Patrick Williamson, for his lifelong model of high spirit, family loyalty, and fortitude.

New York City, 2012

Foreword

Ellen Dunham-Jones

Four hundred sixty and counting. That is 380 more active or pending suburban retrofit projects in our database today than in 2008, when June Williamson and I finished writing *Retrofitting Suburbia* (Hoboken: Wiley, 2009/2011). It's a useful gauge of the context for future change as envisioned in this remarkable book. There has been an encouraging growth in the number of ghostboxes, dead malls, dying commercial corridors, aging office parks, and blighted garden apartment complexes across the United States that have been reinhabited, redeveloped, or regreened into more sustainable places. The expansion of the database has resulted from a number of factors but most importantly points to the very real market dynamics, policy changes, and public support that underlie the hypothetical design propositions presented in this book. Boldly ambitious, unabashedly forward looking, and daring to be systemic, the new visions for tired suburban places shown in *Designing Suburban Futures* are buoyed by a groundswell of change in suburbia. Williamson shows us how suburbia has historically been a site of great experimentation and evolving lifestyles. Today, the suburbs are simply not as suburban as we thought they were, and the proliferation of aging, underperforming suburban properties is providing us with tremendous opportunities to imagine new possibilities that correct for the unintended consequences of the past while better meeting future needs and desires. This book allows us to witness the evolution of third-generation suburban retrofits.

Whereas the first generation of suburban retrofits was largely developer-led, single-parcel examples of urbanization through negotiation in booming markets, the second generation emerged after the 2008 economic crash and is more often led by the public sector. Many municipalities took advantage of the lull in permitting activity to update their regulations and their tools for public–private partnerships to better position themselves for a retrofitted future. Whether in the form of new masterplans to revitalize suburban downtowns or stretches of dying commercial strip corridors, more than 75 communities since 2009 have rezoned and replanned large, multiparcel areas, often in conjunction with transit improvements and ecological repair.

Community buy-in hasn't always been easy. Residents' fears of change and of the incompatibility of the new have often stripped ambitious retrofit plans of their affordable housing components, higher densities, reduced parking requirements, and connections to existing neighborhoods. These fears have often been eased by neotraditional styling and the renewal of civic placemaking techniques. Serving as the sheep's clothing on the suburban public's perception of the wolf of urbanism, these strategies have led to mixed results. Some result in kitschy agglomerations that don't live up to the traditions they reference. Others have integrated uses, scale, details, materials, and landscape into great, beloved places, contributing to greater public interest in retrofits and a greater openness to change. Although the recession has significantly slowed implementation, the combined effect of demographic and generational shifts, Wi-Fi, increased interest in the health benefits of walking and biking, competitive federal grants for sustainable community planning, reduced municipal budgets and concerns about rising gas prices has supported adoption of second-generation retrofits to reduce automobile dependency and accommodate the growing market for more urban lifestyles in suburban areas.

Based on this book's proposals, the ambition to instigate systemic change will be even more pronounced in the third generation of retrofits. Whether tackling metropolitan-scale systems such as transit, aquifer protection, and food and power generation or constructing new community-building processes for the arts, localized production, and collective ownership, these projects operate at an infrastructural scale. Some of them, such as Long Division and LIRR: Long Island Radically Rezoned, seek to fundamentally eradicate the suburban development pattern. However, most of them, exemplified perhaps by SUBHUB Transit System and Bethpage MoMA P.S. 2, seek to augment and intensify the functionality and diversity of suburbia's existing infrastructure and places. Rather than replace suburbia's rigidly separated uses and infrastructures, the proposals come up with inventive ways to connect them into integrated multimodal, mixed-use, shared networks.

Is the willingness to adapt rather than rebuild indicative of a postrecession paradigm shift? We see more attention in these projects to biking and buses than to investments in heavy and light rail. This may be because of Long Island's uniquely extensive existing rail system. But it might also be part of a broader interest in lower-cost alternatives and in pooling resources for shared amenities, in contrast to suburbia's history of insistent private ownership.

Rather than seeing *Designing Suburban Futures* as a cookbook and the projects as discrete recipes, I hope readers will see it instead as a shopping list. Williamson has culled a rich assortment of ingredients that improve by being layered with each other in pungent combinations. But what has to happen to allow the realization of such future dishes?

The biggest obstacles to change are the standards, regulations, and financing practices that have reproduced suburbia for the past 60 years. I'm proud to be chair of the board of the Congress for the New Urbanism (CNU), a leader in reforming the rules of the game so as to better enable realization of alternative suburban futures. Some of the tools that CNU has already developed include LEED for Neighborhood Development (in cooperation with the U.S. Green Building Council and the Natural Resources Defense Council), *Designing Walkable Urban Thoroughfares* (in cooperation with the Institute of Transportation Engineers and the Federal Highway Administration and now a recommended practice for

transportation engineers), the rural-to-urban transect, and the techniques associated with substituting suburbia's use-based zoning codes with form-based codes. All are welcome to join CNU's current initiatives. These include Live/Work/Walk's removal of financial obstacles to urbanism (including raising the U.S. Department of Housing and Urban Development, Fannie Mae, and Freddie Mac caps on mixed use and creating a new mixed-use asset class), Highways to Boulevards, Sustainable Street Networks, and the Sprawl Retrofit Initiative's work on model legislation, community toolkits, and long-term strategies for replacing the current "drive 'til you qualify" default model of affordable housing with housing along suburban commercial corridors that have been retrofitted into attractive transit boulevards.

There is still so much work to be done. Future challenges include changing mortgage underwriting to take location efficiency into account and more thoughtful integration of suburban retrofitting at the regional scale. The greyfield audit produced by the Long Island Index and the Regional Plan Association to undergird the Build a Better Burb competition is an exemplary tool in this regard. Documenting every vacant property and surface parking lot within one half mile of a Long Island Rail Road station or downtown, the audit allows planners and designers to zoom out and identify which sites should be regreened (because we never should have built there in the first place), which should be redeveloped (because of their transit and employment access), and which should be targeted for reinhabitation by entrepreneurial low-profits and community-serving nonprofits. Collectively, the marvelous projects in this book do just that and are exactly the inspiration we need to redesign our suburban future.

Ellen Dunham-Jones is a professor in the School of Architecture at the Georgia Institute of Technology. She is chair of the board of the Congress for the New Urbanism and co-author, with June Williamson, of *Retrofitting Suburbia: Urban Design Solutions for Redesigning Suburbs.*

Introduction

Not only is the city an object which is perceived (and perhaps enjoyed) by millions of people of widely diverse class and character, but it is the product of many builders who are constantly modifying the structure for reasons of their own. While it may be stable in general outlines for some time, it is ever changing in detail. Only partial control can be exercised over its growth and form. There is no final result, only a continuous succession of phases.[1]
– Kevin Lynch, *The Image of the City* (1960)

Compared to the lifespan and the long history of urban settlements, the postwar suburban extensions appear infant creations, not fully developed and lacking articulation of their physical features. These "supernovas" of urban explosions have certainly drawn social attention, but it appears that the scientific community is waiting for "the dust to settle" (sometimes literally) before talking a closer look at this new phenomenon.[2]
– Kiril Stanilov, introduction to *Suburban Form: An International Perspective* (2004)

What will *you* do to design a better, more resilient future for suburbs?

I pose this question in all seriousness. As Kevin Lynch notes, cities are constantly being modified by a range of urban actors, resulting in continuous transformations of growth and form. If you, reading this, are an architect, a planner, a politician, a teacher, a student, or simply an interested resident, you are one of these urban actors,

playing a role in the building of our metropolises. But, as Kiril Stanilov suggests, suburbs, particularly the postwar extensions, appear to be "infant creations" and are often excluded from the urban imagination and discourse surrounding cities, sustainability, and urban resilience. However, suburbs are key components – some might say dominant components – of urbanized regions throughout the globe, especially in the land-rich developed nations of North America, and in Europe.

Urban resiliency is the need for urban systems to be reconceived and designed to have improved capacity to withstand disturbances, including climate change, natural disasters, terrorism, and energy insecurity, without breaking down.[3] Resilience thinking must be applied vigorously to the explosive suburban "supernovas" Stanilov describes, even as we struggle to understand their basic morphological properties of growth and form. These are concurrent projects. Investments in suburban resiliency will lead to better places to live, places that can provide more security in the face of global climate change and improved physical and emotional health, places that promote mobility and ease of movement within higher-density nodes and corridors, places with better, fresher food, places with more energy choices and resources, greater affordability, and more awareness of the local bioregion and the roles humans play in shaping and stewarding it.[4]

As of their latest censuses, the populations of the United States and Canada are both more than 80 percent urbanized.[5] But about half of North Americans in these countries live in suburban settings, predominantly in the types of sprawling urbanism that were dominant in the latter half of the twentieth century, characterized by a low-density settlement form, with separated land uses and overwhelmingly dependent on private automobiles for transportation. Using satellite imagery, census data, and historical maps, researchers affiliated with the Lincoln Institute of Land Policy recently reported a five-fold decline in average tract density in U.S. cities between 1910 and 2000.[6] This means that as cities grew in population, they spread out at a much faster rate. For example, the Chicago metro area shifted from 19 people per acre in 1945 to fewer than 7 people per acre in 2000.[7] This choice of settlement form and the lifestyles associated with it have a very high ecological cost: Americans and Canadians make up just about 5 percent of the world's population but by many measures are responsible for a vastly disproportionate amount of greenhouse gas (GHG) emissions.[8] Several other countries – throughout Europe and Latin America and in Japan – are similarly urbanized, though not quite as sprawling in settlement form and per capita land consumption.

At the beginning of the twenty-first century much of the rest of the world is playing a high-stakes game of development and urbanization catch-up; large populations throughout Asia, especially, but also in Africa are observed to be migrating from rural to urban areas at rapid rates, often without adequate planning.[9] Per capita GHG emissions are increasing precipitously in many of these regions. Furthermore, these regions contain many places highly susceptible to the weather disruptions anticipated by climate change models, such as drought, severe storms, and coastal flooding, with huge populations at risk.

Well-designed and well-managed urban settlement forms are increasingly understood to hold a key to solutions proffered for managing the twenty-first century's sustainability crises.[10] However, the global urbanization processes now unfolding in countries such as China, India, and Indonesia – which together constitute 40 percent of the current world population of almost seven billion – are in a phase of adding substantially to the strains on the earth's resources and ecological systems. The urbanized areas in these countries are growing faster in land area than in population, indicating that average urban densities are *decreasing* across the globe as aspects of North American settlement forms are adopted across the globe.[11] This should be extremely worrisome.

Urban–Suburban Reciprocity

In urban form and development in North America at the beginning of the twenty-first century a reciprocal process is occurring between North American center cities and their suburbs. Center cities, where about one third of the population currently lives, a percentage that has remained steady for 70 years, are observed to be suburbanizing through the proliferation of standardized development types such as big box chain stores. (However, these stores have adapted to more traditional urban morphologies of smaller blocks and higher street walls by building vertically.) At the same time, urbanized areas located outside these center cities are experiencing increased densification and diversification of nodes and corridors, in the beginnings of a systemic process of suburban retrofitting.[12] In our book *Retrofitting Suburbia*, Ellen Dunham-Jones and I coined the term *incremental metropolitanism* to refer to a polycentric vision that could be advanced by the retrofitting of appropriate sites, both by densifying and diversifying nodes along transit-served corridors and by *de*-densifying other, failed sites for ecological repair.

Various dynamics drive suburban retrofitting in North America, and these drivers have only intensified since the 2007 onset of the Great Recession:

– Combating the contribution of GHG emissions to climate change entails reducing the high carbon footprints of suburban dwellers, up to three times higher than those of center city dwellers, due to driving and energy-inefficient detached dwellings.[13]

– Increased acknowledgment of the eventual approach of "peak oil" conditions, coupled with the fluctuating but overall rising price of gasoline at the pump.

– Demographic change in suburbs, primarily because of longer life spans and the aging of the baby boom generation, leading to a smaller and decreasing percentage of households with children. Change is also caused by the proliferation of immigrant gateway suburbs and a pronounced rise in suburban poverty. North American suburbs are much more varied and diverse than generally assumed.[14]

– Aging of the physical fabric of the "first suburbs" – the communities built out in the postwar era of mass suburbanization from the 1940s to the 1960s – especially of cheaply built commercial properties. There is an overabundance of "underperforming asphalt" in our over-retailed suburban landscapes, land that could and should be used to reshape North America.[15]

Suburbs contain millions of acres of land that is currently vacant or dedicated to asphalt-covered surface parking lots. Much of this paved greyfield land surrounds regional shopping malls, big box stores, and industrial parks, but a significant portion is in older suburban

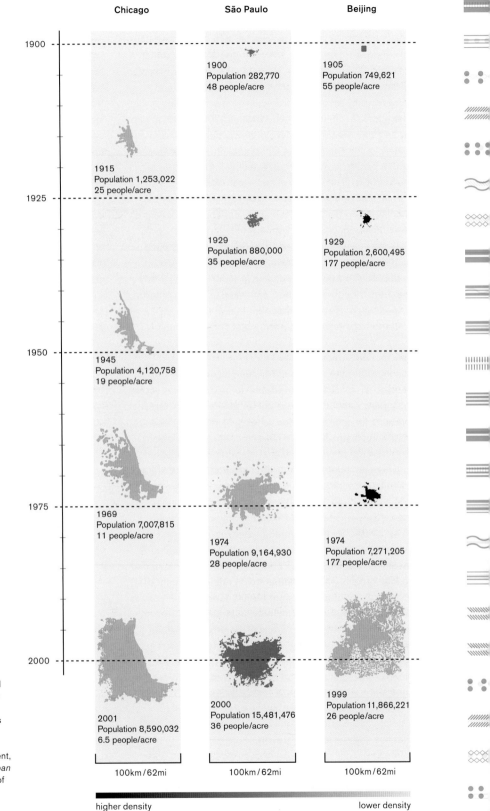

| Chicago | São Paulo | Beijing |

1900

1900
Population 282,770
48 people/acre

1905
Population 749,621
55 people/acre

1915
Population 1,253,022
25 people/acre

1925

1929
Population 880,000
35 people/acre

1929
Population 2,600,495
177 people/acre

1945
Population 4,120,758
19 people/acre

1950

1969
Population 7,007,815
11 people/acre

1975

1974
Population 9,164,930
28 people/acre

1974
Population 7,271,205
177 people/acre

2000

1999
Population 11,866,221
26 people/acre

2001
Population 8,590,032
6.5 people/acre

2000
Population 15,481,476
36 people/acre

100km / 62mi   100km / 62mi   100km / 62mi

higher density   lower density

Twentieth-Century Urbanization Trends.
As metropolitan populations grew, urban land
area tended to expand at a greater rate, often
resulting in much lower overall urban population densities. Will twenty-first-century trends
follow suit?

Source: Based on data from Angel, S., J. Parent,
D. L. Civco, and A. M. Blei, 2012. *Atlas of Urban
Expansion*, Cambridge MA: Lincoln Institute of
Land Policy.

downtowns, places that languished in the second half of the twentieth century. This downtown asphalt is also, perhaps not surprisingly, often adjacent to transit infrastructure built before the automobile age, such as the Long Island Rail Road, New Jersey Transit, and Metro-North commuter rail systems in the suburbs of New York City.

A Call to Action

Designing Suburban Futures is written as an urgent response to the documented ecological, environmental, social, and economic problems of the dominant types of sprawling suburban form. It is a call to action for robust yet sensitive innovations in architectural, urban, and landscape design to achieve future resiliency in the aging and outdated suburbs of North America. These spread-out regions dwarfing central cities are where the majority of the population works and lives, as confirmed in the United States by the 2000 Census; these are the landscapes that most need transformative attention. Similar challenges confront other postindustrial economies with ecologically and economically stressed and aging peripheral settlements. Globalizing economies in China, India, Brazil, and elsewhere risk repeating the same mistakes as they undergo rapid urbanization; planners, designers, and developers everywhere can learn valuable lessons by examining innovative design responses to North American conditions, such as those produced for the ideas competitions and exhibitions documented and discussed in this volume.

In North America, urban expansion as usual – that is, through real estate growth machines promoting ever more car-dependent, low-density suburbanization, often in high-risk locations – will no longer work in the future, even if one blindly chooses to disregard the high ecological costs. Economically and demographically, the playing field is shifting decisively. As Richard Florida reminds us, "Historically, America's economic growth has hinged on its ability to create new development patterns, new economic landscapes that simultaneously expand space and intensify our use of it."[16] Statistical indicators show that North American suburban regions are facing several pressing challenges that could spur innovation and, perhaps, entirely new interpretations of the very concept of economic growth. Some of these challenges are shared in common throughout the continent, and others are particular to the specifics of sociopolitical and economic dynamics and the local bioregion.

For New York's Long Island region, waterlocked and seemingly built out, the primary challenges are to build affordable housing and provide greater housing choice, especially for rentals in multiunit buildings; to bring diverse communities together in a shared public realm; to improve equity and access to opportunity for all in a context of fractured governance in which de facto racial and ethnic segregation is stubbornly persistent; to increase transit mobility options and reduce traffic congestion and fossil fuel dependence; to meet the needs of retiring baby boomers who want to age in place; to fight the "brain drain" of younger residents who don't see a future and leave; to preserve remaining open space and natural resources; and to manage a lengthy, developed coastline at increasing risk from flooding and sea level rise.

Suburban regions across the United States face related challenges. For the Pikes Peak region, around Colorado Springs south of Denver, the indicators suggest some trends that are similar, such as an increase in the median age as longevity increases and young people tend to leave and make their lives elsewhere, and the significant mismatch between household types – increasingly diverse in size and type – and housing options. The housing stock is three quarters single-family detached and mobile homes. Other trends, both troubling and hopeful, are different: Subdivisions are at risk from wildfires, rates of child poverty and homelessness are rising, mass transit service is declining while housing and transportation cost burdens on households are increasing,[17] but the quantity of cycling and pedestrian trails is growing, both for recreation and for commuting to work.[18]

Two simple points have been guides to my advocacy work. First, it may be that the greatest gains in urban resiliency are to be made in suburbs. Vast potential exists for transformations both subtle and profound. Second, close study of the past, present, and future potential of suburban forms in already hyperurbanized regions offers valuable cautionary tales and illuminating lessons for currently urbanizing places across the globe.

Build a Better Burb

More than two hundred ideas submitted in 2010 to the Build a Better Burb urban design competition demonstrate the potential for incremental metropolitanism in the eastern suburbs of New York City, on Long Island, home to nearly three million residents. I had the honor to help conceive and organize the competition for the nonprofit Long Island Index, an organization that has undertaken a decade's worth of indicator studies to track the performance of the region according to several metrics: economy, health, education, environment, governance, and communities.[19] The Index had commissioned a study from the Regional

Plan Association of the amount of vacant land and surface parking lots within a half mile of 156 downtowns and commuter rail stations in the 1,300-square-mile region, comprising Nassau and Suffolk counties.[20] They mapped an astonishing 8,300 acres of greyfield opportunity in just these locations, roughly equivalent to the land area of Manhattan south of 50th Street – an astonishingly valuable and productive piece of urban land. Or, to provide a different comparison, these scattered, downtown greyfields are equivalent in area to eighty regional shopping malls.

The competition asked designers to envision bold ideas for this underused land, to propose new uses and forms that might address the many challenges the region is facing as it matures and transitions – one must fervently hope – toward a resilient future. The proposals of two dozen finalists illustrated a range of fascinating, innovative ideas, suggesting several intriguing new directions for suburban futures, such as using under-capacity commuter and school buses for local freight transport, moving office parks to downtowns and converting vacated land to intensive organic farms, intensifying the construction of accessory dwelling units in residential neighborhoods, reintroducing the shop–house typology, sequestering carbon in highway verges and just about everywhere else, protecting freshwater aquifers, chopping up malls and putting housing on top, vastly expanding biking, and figuring out clever bottom-up ways to pay for it all.

This book reports and reflects on the compelling results of the competition as examples for designing better suburban futures. Some of the predominant themes and ideas that emerged from the competition are the critical importance of considering freshwater and carbon systems and the need to robustly reintroduce agriculture to suburban land use regimes, to provide multiple transit alternatives, to reimagine financing, and to provide a plethora of solutions to the pressing need for housing diversity and nodes of increased density to increase urban efficiency and resiliency.

Since the competition's winners were announced in October 2010, the Long Island Index has transformed Build a Better Burb into an ongoing project, supported by a steady stream of new content on a redesigned website and other social media sites. It is a concerted, direct effort to raise awareness in the general public about the documented challenges that suburban region faces and to get productive conversations going about potential solutions through design and planning, engendered by the competition and demonstrated by realized projects – exemplary case studies – from other regions. The goal is to neutralize, perhaps even convert and engage, the obstructive NIMBY (not-in-my-backyard) mindset.[21]

On the night of October 29, 2012 suburban risk was brought to the fore by the ravages of Hurricane Sandy, a storm that slammed the shores of the northeastern United States. The hurricane, combined with a nor'easter winter storm and a lunar high tide, compounded by sea level rise (measured at roughly 1 foot over the past century in New York City), resulted in an unprecedented storm surge that caused devastating flooding, death and destruction, lengthy power outages, infrastructure disruptions, and gasoline shortages in the heavily suburbanized megaregion. Long Island was hit particularly hard. The full impact of Sandy is yet to be calculated, but it is likely to be transformative.

Designing Suburban Futures

Two parts make up this book: the first part provides the contextual vision for dramatic suburban change and highlights design opportunities and emerging strategies for achieving suburban resilience, and the second part comprehensively presents an exemplar for the vision by reporting on the best schemes submitted in the highly successful Build a Better Burb competition. This book provides an important new resource that I hope will be an inspiration for the many other places across the continent, and the globe, facing parallel challenges to those confronted by America's self-styled "first suburb," Long Island. As goes the suburbs, so go we all.

It is my hope that from reading this book you might get new ideas for what you can do to help design a better, more resilient future for all suburbs, everywhere. Change is not only possible, change is necessary.

Notes

1. Kevin Lynch, *The Image of the City* (Cambridge, MA: MIT Press, 1960), 2.

2. Kiril Stanilov, "Introduction: Postwar Growth and Suburban Development Patterns," in Kiril Stanilov and Brenda Case Scheer, eds., *Suburban Form: An International Perspective* (New York: Routledge, 2004), 4.

3. William E. Rees, co-originator of ecological footprint analysis, maintains that to do so, urban development strategies "must abandon efficiency and maximization as primary goals in favor of social equity and ecological stability." William E. Rees, "Thinking Resilience," in Richard Heinberg and Daniel Lerch, eds., *The Post Carbon Reader: Managing the 21st Century Sustainability Crises* (Healdsburg, CA: Watershed Media, 2010), 3–40.

4. Peter Newman, Timothy Beatley, and Heather Boyer, *Resilient Cities: Responding to Peak Oil and Climate Change* (Washington, DC: Island Press, 2009), 11.

5. Number for United States from United States 2010 Census: http://2010.census.gov/2010census/. For Canada, Canada 2011 Census: http://www.statcan.gc.ca.

6. Shlomo Angel, Jason Parent, Daniel L. Civco, and Alejandro M. Blei, "The Persistent Decline in Urban Densities: Global and Historical Evidence of 'Sprawl,'" Cambridge, MA: Lincoln Institute of Land Policy Working Paper, July 2010.

7. Shlomo Angel, Jason Parent, Daniel L. Civco, and Alejandro M. Blei, *Atlas of Urban Expansion* (Cambridge, MA: Lincoln Institute of Land Policy, 2012). Online at http://www.lincolninst.edu/subcenters /atlas-urban-expansion/.

8. In 2012, the U.S. population was estimated to be 313.5 million, Canada's was 34.7 million, and the overall world population was estimated to be 7.012 billion. Estimates from the World Resources Institute show the following rates of greenhouse gas emissions per capita for the year 2000: 23 tonnes in North America, 3.9 in China, and 1.8 in India. See http://cait.wri.org/.

9. World Urbanization Prospects, the 2011 Revision, from the United Nations, Department of Economic and Social Affairs, Population Division, Population Estimates and Projections Section, http://esa.un.org/unpd /wup/index.html. Though useful for macro comparisons, the UN data must be approached with some caution, as they depend on self-reporting from individual countries on the percentages of their populations that are urban. Definitions vary somewhat from country to country.

10. For example, see Warren Karlenzig, "The Death of Sprawl: Designing Urban Resilience for the Twenty-First-Century Resource and Climate Crisis," in Heinberg and Lerch, 295–313. See also Newman, Beatley, and Boyer, *Resilient Cities*.

11. Angel et al., "The Persistent Decline in Urban Densities."

12. Ellen Dunham-Jones and June Williamson, *Retrofitting Suburbia: Urban Design Solutions for Redesigning Suburbs*, updated edition (Hoboken, NJ: Wiley, 2011).

13. The rate for carbon dioxide equivalent emissions in New York City was measured at 7.1 metric tons per capita in 2007, less than one third of the national average of 24.5. San Francisco's rate was 11.2. New York City Mayor's Office of Long-Term Planning and Sustainability, "Inventory of New York City Greenhouse Gas Emissions," City of New York, April 2007. Online at http://www.nyc.gov/html/om/pdf /ccp_report041007.pdf.

14. See various reports from the State of Metropolitan America effort at the Brookings Institution. Online at http://www.brookings.edu/about /programs/metro/stateofmetroamerica. See also Bernadette Hanlon, John Rennie Short, and Thomas J. Vicino, *Cities and Suburbs: New Metropolitan Realities in the US* (New York: Routledge: 2010).

15. Arthur C. Nelson, *Reshaping Metropolitan America: Development Trends and Opportunities to 2030* (Washington, DC: Island Press, 2013). See also Nelson, "Leadership in a New Era," *Journal of the American Planning Association* 72:4(Autumn 2006):393–407.

16. Richard Florida, "Foreword," in *Retrofitting Suburbia: Urban Design Solutions for Redesigning Suburbs*.

17. For more on the effect of transportation cost burdens on households across the United States, see the Center for Neighborhood Technology's online H+T Affordability Index: http://www.cnt.org/tcd/ht.

18. I served on an AIA Sustainable Design Assessment Team (SDAT) for the Pikes Peak region in 2011. My section of the final report was heavily influenced by the Quality of Life Indicators for the Pikes Peak Region yearly reports, sponsored by the Pikes Peak United Way, which can be accessed at http://www.ppunitedway.org/. The AIA SDAT final report is available at http://www.aia.org/aiaucmp/groups/aia/documents/pdf /aiab092909.pdf.

19. For background on the Long Island Index, see http://www.long islandindex.org/. For ongoing content related to the Build a Better Burb project, including material on the competition, see http://www.builda betterburb.org/.

20. Regional Plan Association, "Places to Grow, an Analysis of the Potential for Transit-Accessible Housing and Jobs in Long Island's Downtown and Station Areas," Long Island Index Report, 2010. Online at http://www.longislandindex.org/2010.711.0.html.

21. The Long Island Index's director, Ann Golob, reports findings that there is now general acceptance of the trend of outward migration of young people (aged 18–35) and increased understanding that downtowns are important to redressing the problem. Interview with author, June 7, 2012.

UNTITLED II, Nevada 2010, Christoph Gielen.

UNTITLED X, Nevada 2010, Christoph Gielen.

OUTER HOUSTON II, Texas 2006, Christoph Gielen.

OUTER HOUSTON III, Texas 2006, Christoph Gielen.

New York-based artist Christoph Gielen specializes in photographic aerial studies of urban development in its relation to land use, exploring the intersection of art and environmental politics.

Vision: A Role for Design in Suburban Resilience

Context for Change

Those who cannot remember the past are condemned
to repeat it.
–George Santayana, *Reason in Common Sense* (1905)

The trajectory of urbanization and industrialization in North America from the mid-nineteenth century to the turn of the twenty-first was phenomenal. The majority of North Americans lived in suburbs in the year 2000, as U.S. and Canadian census data show, even more in neighborhoods characterized by suburban form: generally low-density, use-separated, and car-dependent places.[1]

But back in 1850 the continent was still overwhelmingly rural and agricultural, with fewer than 10 percent of the U.S. population living in metropolitan areas, comprised of cities together with adjacent suburbs. The country became predominantly urban rather than rural sometime in the 1940s, with about 33 percent of the population living in center cities at that time and 17 percent in suburbs, a roughly 2:1 ratio. (The world's overall population has more recently crossed this threshold, driven by massive rural to urban migration in populous China, India, and elsewhere.)

Today, the U.S. population remains around 30 percent in cities, but the share in suburbs has grown to more than 50 percent, or more if the more than 550 "micropolitan" urban areas defined for the last census are included. (Micropolitan Statistical Areas, defined as areas based around an urban cluster of 10,000 to 49,999 residents, were included for the first time in the U.S. 2010 Census. These areas, 576 in the last census, account for an additional 10 percent of the population that may be considered nonrural.) All the urbanization that occurred since the 1940s, since the United States passed the 50 percent threshold of urbanization, has, in a macro sense, been suburbanization.[2]

Of course, each individual metropolitan area has experienced a particular trajectory of growth, with some city centers hollowing out, the middle class decanting into surrounding suburbs for a troubling, complex set of push and pull reasons, as in Detroit and Cleveland. Others, such as New York and Chicago, have held stable in the center while the overall metro area grew in population, but even more so in land area. And yet others, such as Phoenix and Houston, have grown rapidly in recent decades in a "flat" manner such that the urbanism of the center is hardly distinguishable from that of the suburbs.

We might also note that many of those who live in cities, that is, within the municipal boundaries of cities, which vary greatly in extent depending on each city's historical approach to annexation, inhabit settings that are suburban in formal character – in detached houses, with little or no mass transit. Residents of these neighborhoods may be unable to pass the quart of milk test: They are not within walking distance of anything nonresidential, not even a convenience store. The generally low-density, use-separated, and dispersed character of this urbanization is crucial to keep in mind when considering the rural to urban migration now occurring in many populations throughout the globe as people respond en masse to the upheavals of rapidly

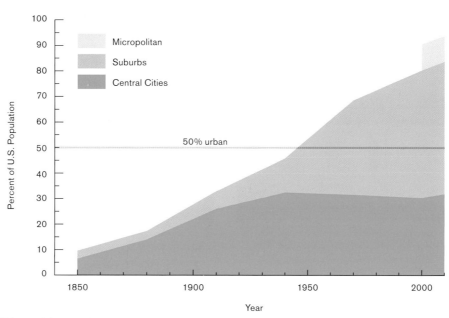

Percentage of total U.S. population living in urbanized areas and in their central cities and suburbs, 1850 to 2010. The percentage of the population in central cities has remained constant, at around 30 percent, since the 1940s, while the population share in suburbs has steadily grown.

Sources: U.S. Census of Population, 1910 to 2010; Becky M. Nicolaides and Andrew Wiese, "Introduction," *The Suburb Reader*, 2006, 2.

industrializing economies. Although the suburbanization of land-rich developed countries in the twentieth century was accompanied by a remarkable rise in public health, societal wealth, and quality of life, it came at a significant ecological cost, the extent of which we are only now beginning to grasp in its entirety. How will this global process unfold in the current century? What useful lessons are offered by the North American experience?

Although Americans and Canadians make up a little less than 5 percent of the world's overall population, North Americans from these countries are responsible for a vastly disproportionate amount of greenhouse gas (GHG) emissions. Industrializing and urbanization trends in other regions of the globe suggest that their populations may be starting to catch up in rates of GHG emissions per capita, creating a collision course with population growth. The risks are exacerbated when currently urbanizing populations choose to pursue, even in part, predominant North American models of realizing the dream of owning a detached home. Not only are these models unnecessarily high in both land and resource consumption per capita, but they also have tended to produce, over time, persistent conditions of unequal access to opportunity, contradicting the initial promises of the dream.

This chapter is a compact, illustrated history of North American suburbanization, as viewed through six successive historical paradigms that exerted strong influences on the varied suburban landscapes that dominate the continent today. First is the *pastoral paradigm* of the nineteenth century; second, the transit-served rise of *streetcar suburbs*; third, the *visionary schemes* and experiments of the early twentieth century; fourth, the establishment of the mechanisms and protocols for *building and selling the dream*; fifth, the *cul-de-sac paradigm* of the post–World War II boom; and, finally, the environmental ravages of the late twentieth-century *paradigm of sprawl*.

By remembering and analyzing the forces that shaped the past, we can seek and find useful tools to help shape a better future.

An examination of U.S. Census data indicates that the share of the overall population in center cities has remained steady at waround one third for at least 70 years. Will this proportion change significantly in coming decades? Probably not, especially with increasing longevity. Americans are living longer, *much* longer.

Laura Carstensen, director of the Stanford Center on Longevity, recounts how U.S. life

Study for a Simple Country House (left) and *Bracketed Cottage with Ornamental Veranda*, 1842, Alexander Jackson Davis. Collection of the New-York Historical Society. A. J. Davis and A. J. Downing were influential tastemakers of their time, producing house and estate designs for country gentlemen, offering varied styles to suit the character of the owner, with symmetry and plain lines for commonsense men, ornament and cozy nooks for men of feeling.

expectancy jumped dramatically, from 47 years to 77 years, over the course of the twentieth century. This gain surpasses all previous gains in the history of human evolution combined.[3] It is simply astonishing. It is estimated that by 2050 the U.S. population over 65 will double, to more than eighty million, growing at a much more rapid rate than overall population growth.

And these older people, who will be living many decades past their child-rearing years, will be living longer in the suburban communities where they already live, with the exception of some who will move into center cities. In the suburbs they must drive to everything. How will our culture and society adapt?

Pastoral Paradigm

The earliest historical suburban paradigm in this story, dating to the mid-nineteenth century, is the *pastoral*, the concept that in the face of rapid industrialization of cities, a more moral life could be created outside the city's limits, in country places where landscapes — be they wild or agricultural — could be tamed to picturesque ideals, molded in the service of the domestic realm. Chief proponents were brilliant landscape designer Andrew Jackson Downing and influential domestic feminist Catharine Beecher, both of whom published best-selling house guides in this period.[4]

Downing, who might have designed the Mall in Washington, D.C. and New York's Central Park had he not

died tragically in a Hudson River ferry accident in 1852, when he was just 36, was a celebrated but self-made taste-maker, as was his architect colleague Alexander Jackson Davis. Both are comparable in their influence to Robert A. M. Stern or Ralph Lauren today. Downing operated from a home base north of New York City, in the towns and hamlets of Westchester County, where he developed and published schemes for "improving" working farmland into picturesque country estates. He sought to promote Republican virtues of self-reliance, by grafting them onto a vision of the responsibilities to the land of elite country gentlemen, borrowed from England and the influential writings of British horticulturist and landscape designer John Claudius Loudon.

Beecher, the eldest daughter of Transcendentalist preacher Lyman Beecher, a favorite on the antebellum lecture circuit, was perhaps more like Martha Stewart; she was a shrewd and ambitious woman who made her name extolling the virtues of excelling in the domestic arts. Though she herself never married, the domestic brand of feminism she espoused depended on protecting the gendered role of women as morally superior beings, uniquely qualified by their greater capacity for self-sacrifice for the responsibilities of child rearing and household management. Her model house plans were pretty nifty, including perhaps the earliest prototype of a streamlined, single-surface, rationally planned kitchen.[5]

The Hudson River School painting *The Lackawanna Valley*, painted in 1856 by George Inness, exemplifies American ambivalence in this period toward what cultural

The Lackawanna Valley, c. 1856. Oil on canvas. George Inness. Inness's painting exemplifies the mid-nineteenth-century pastoral paradigm described by Leo Marx as "the machine in the garden."

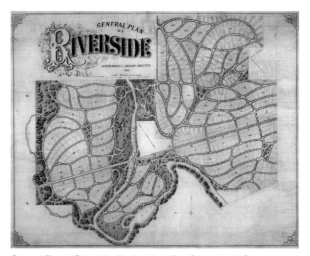

General Plan of Riverside, Illinois, 1869, F. L. Olmsted and Calvert Vaux. This plan, with its teardrop-shaped blocks and picturesque park, set an aspirational standard for planning residential suburbs.

historian Leo Marx memorably called "the machine in the garden."[6] In the painting, a steam train cuts diagonally across a middle landscape recently clear-cut and littered with stumps. Manufactory buildings in the distance also expel smoke, though it is white and puffy, not at all ominous. In the foreground, a reclining figure in a straw hat sits contemplating the scene, a classic pastoral landscape, drastically altered in his lifetime but still mostly lush and green. The scene is reminiscent of a descriptive passage by Nathaniel Hawthorne that Marx analyzes, of a place in Concord, Massachusetts called Sleepy Hollow. The passage is from unpublished notes Hawthorne wrote in the summer of 1844:

> But, hark! There is the whistle of the locomotive – the long shriek, harsh, above all other harshness, for the space of a mile cannot mollify it into harmony. It tells a story of busy men, citizens, from the hot street, who have come to spend a day in a country village, men of business; in short of all unquietness; and no wonder that it gives such a startling shriek, since it brings the noisy world into the midst of our slumbrous peace. As our thoughts repose again, after this interruption, we find ourselves gazing up at the leaves, and comparing their different aspect, the beautiful diversity of green…[7]

Soon, the idea of the pastoral country estate, where a man might retreat with his family from the stresses of the industrializing city, was expanded to visions for pastoral communities of like-minded families. An early example is Riverside, Illinois, the iconic planned railroad suburb laid out as a speculative endeavor on swampy land for the Riverside Improvement Company in 1869 by Frederick Law Olmsted, during his partnership with Calvert Vaux. Its distinctive teardrop blocks and fenceless yards were designed to create the illusion of living in a large, leafy park. Olmsted is on record as quite bullish on suburbs, claiming, "No town can long survive without great suburbs."[8] Almost half of the land at Riverside was set aside for a passive park, designed to manage stormwater. Planned suburbs soon boasted lawns for active leisure sports such as croquet, tennis, and golf.

In recent years, before the housing market collapse of the late 2000s, the "bourgeois utopia" of the leisure-oriented suburban enclave was visibly alive and well, as evidenced by the practice of "McMansioning," or tearing down perfectly serviceable but modest houses to build bigger ones, and the exurban development of grotesquely scaled-up gated subdivisions.[9] Photographer Angela Strassheim captured the pastoral mood – at once both evangelical and exclusive – in her image of Elsa, a tanned, fit woman gazing out vacantly in a pink dressing gown from a sumptuous lawn and supersized manse.

In 1981, historian Dolores Hayden, producer of seminal scholarship explaining the contributions and contradictions of domestic feminists such as Catharine Beecher and her contemporaries, published the provocative essay "What Would a Non-Sexist City Be Like?"[10] She called for

Untitled (Elsa), 2003, Angela Strassheim.

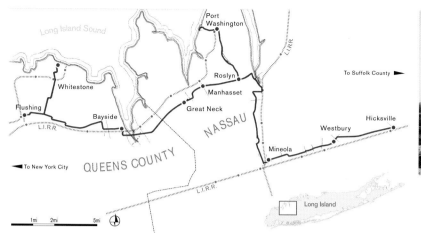

The New York and North Shore Traction Company built and operated a streetcar line, long since demolished, from Flushing, in Queens, to Hicksville, in Nassau County, opening up acres of land to suburban development along the 30-mile (48-kilometer) route. Source: Map redrawn from Vincent F. Seyfried, New York and North Shore Traction Company, 1956.

an attack on the conventional division between public and private space, especially in suburbs, with the aim of transforming "the sexual division of domestic labor, the privatized economic basis of domestic work, and the spatial separation of homes and workplaces." A generation later the question remains a provocation. What does a non-sexist city look like? Have we achieved it anywhere yet, and if so, where?

A decade later, architect Peter Rowe, in his classic *Making a Middle Landscape*, called for the invigoration of modern pastoralism, which he described as a merger between the pastoral per-spective and a modern technical orientation, as a route toward the creation of an American "poetic of the middle landscape."[11] Can, or should, efforts to merge the pastoral and the technological be reinvigorated today? If so, how?

Streetcar Paradigm

A transportation revolution occurred in the late nineteenth century as amazing new technologies facilitated the expansion and decentralization of the walking city, tripling the reach of commuters and dramatically altering pat-terns of urban development. This revolution facilitated the emergence of the figure of the commuter, named for the discounted or "commuted" fares offered as an enticement to frequent riders. It also ushered in the *streetcar suburb*.

In his groundbreaking book *The Crabgrass Frontier*, his-torian Kenneth Jackson dubbed it "The Time of the Trolley." Once safely electrified, the new trolleys became one of the most rapidly accepted technological innovations in human history. In 1890, there were 1,260 miles of electrified track; by 1903, the number of track miles had jumped to 30,000. The systems were built with route franchises, granted by local municipalities. As a consequence, historian Henry Binford asserts, "the exceptional trip became ordinary."[12]

People of all classes were happy to flee the chaos and crowding of downtown neighborhoods. Streetcars opened up vast areas for development, mostly in a distinctive gridded and connected pattern of closely spaced houses. Streetcar subdivisions were not thought to be picturesque. The buildouts sprouted up on land often owned by the same speculators who constructed the streetcar lines. These men stood to make a tidy profit, though not without risk. Streetcar magnates such as "Borax" Smith in Oakland, Henry Huntington in Pasadena, and Senator Newlands in Washington, D.C. amassed huge fortunes in this heady period through a confluence of interests in transit, land, water, and political influence peddling.

A ring of settlement around North American cities resulted, built in a patchwork pattern of street grids and wood frame houses of various types that facilitated direct access by foot for all residents to the lifeblood of transit. In recently built auto-dependent residential subdivisions this type of street connectivity is sorely lacking. Meanwhile, North American streetcar and interurban lines were almost completely dismantled and discarded by 1960.

– New transit technologies
– Streetcar magnates
– Impact on development patterns

– Sorting by class
– Federal Highway Act of 1916
– Interstate Highway Act of 1956

Dr. David O'Donnell and His Family in 1911 Ford Model T. From weekend leisure conveyance for the whole family to the technology depended on for most daily transportation needs, the availability and affordability of private automobiles transformed North American urbanization in the twentieth century.

Is there a viable future in human-powered transit? The pedaled Shweeb, from New Zealand, is one proposal, though for the present just a novelty.

The culprit? We could blame the private automobile, such as Henry Ford's Model T, introduced in 1908. Ford's innovations in production and pricing made this new technology widely available and affordable. Then, with the Federal Highway Act of 1916 and the Interstate Highway Act of 1956, the United States built an expansive, federally financed infrastructure to support it. Provincial governments were largely responsible for the construction of regional expressways in Canada in the 1960s and 1970s, after the initial postwar boom. The love affair continues unabated to this day. In technological terms, a century is a very long period of time; as a technology, private automobiles seem to have accrued lasting power.

In his thought-provoking handbook *Seven Rules for Sustainable Communities*, Patrick M. Condon estimates that 40 percent of urban residents in the United States and Canada still live in areas once served by streetcars. "In these neighborhoods," he asserts, "alternatives to the car are still available and buildings are inherently more energy efficient (due to shared walls, wind protection and smaller average unit sizes). Most of these districts are still pedestrian and transit friendly, although with rare exception the streetcar and interurban rail lines that once served them have been removed."[13] Condon marshals convincing evidence in support of modern streetcars over other transportation modes; streetcars are energy efficient and reduce pollution, offer a smoother ride, add capacity, and cost less per passenger mile than other mass transit systems.[14]

Many people continue to place great faith in new technologies to help us escape the current environmental predicament of global warming and climate change, brought about in no small part by the fossil fuel appetites of the automobile. We continue to struggle with developing new private mobility or vehicle technologies that could supplant the car: Jetsons jetpacks, Segways, or private rapid transit. One intriguing newcomer is the human-powered Shweeb. Will any of these technologies prove capable of breaking out of the novelty category?

Can the streetcar paradigm of dense and diverse linear corridors be successfully revived in pre-1940s neighborhoods, where millions already live? Or have our daily travel needs become too diffuse and dispersed throughout the metropolis for a fixed network to suffice? What would be needed in exchange for a large percentage of our population to give up their cars? Or, at the very least, their second, third, and fourth household vehicles?

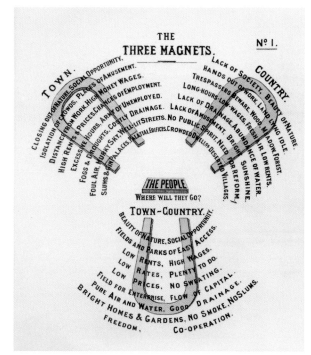

The Three Magnets, 1902, from Ebenezer Howard, *Garden Cities of To-Morrow*. The concept behind Howard's socialist utopian scheme to relieve squalor and overcrowding in urbanizing, industrializing European cities promised people the best of both the town and the country. It has become a recurring visionary theme.

Radburn, New Jersey, 1928, Clarence Stein and Henry Wright. Though never completed, Radburn introduced Howard's ideas to North America. In an attempt to tame and manage traffic by providing separate "foot ways" and "motor ways," Stein and Wright helped innovate the contemporary suburban cul-de-sac.

Visionary Paradigms

What were architects and planners dreaming up during the headiest period of industrialization and urbanization in the United States and Europe? A potent mix of *visionary paradigms* for urban decentralization.

The ideas of utopian socialist and bureaucrat Ebenezer Howard, published in Britain in 1902 in the slim volume *Garden Cities of To-Morrow*, have proved enduringly influential as a planning framework for redirecting urban growth into smaller, satellite settlements. His diagrammatic concept was to combine the advantages of both town and country while mitigating the ills of overcrowding, poverty, and disease by establishing what he called a "new magnet": cooperatively owned garden cities of around 32,000 residents living on 1,000 acres, supported by a compact zone of cottage industries, surrounded by a 5,000-acre agricultural greenbelt. Garden cities would feature "bright homes & gardens, no smoke, no slums." Tantalizingly, he promised his followers a new life of "freedom and co-operation," along with "low rents" and "high wages."[15] Who wouldn't be tempted by this vision?

Howard's garden city ideals were imported to North America and tamed into a design and planning alternative to streetcar subdivisions, which many deemed monotonous, dreary, and substandard. Planners Clarence Stein and Henry Wright, members along with Lewis Mumford of the progressive Regional Planning Association of America, articulated the need for new towns designed specifically "for the motor age." Their aim was to develop settlement patterns configured not to celebrate automotive culture, as was the vision soon to be associated with Le Corbusier and his colleagues in the Congrès Internationaux d'Architecture Moderne, but to put cars in their place.

Stein and Wright's 1928 superblock idea for Radburn, New Jersey eliminated gridiron rectangular blocks. Specialized roads were designed and built for one use instead of all uses, resulting in separate service lanes for direct access to buildings feeding into collector roads around the superblocks, which led to highways. A system of footways and bicycle paths, grade separated from the collector roads, connected to and through the large, shared open green parks in the center of each superblock. To achieve complete separation of pedestrian and automobile, the houses were "turned around," with living and sleeping areas facing the parks and service rooms – kitchens and garages – facing the access lanes.

– Garden Cities of To-Morrow *(Ebenezer Howard)*
– *Regional Planning Association of America*
– *The Radburn Idea (Clarence Stein and Henry Wright)*
– *Broadacre City (F. L. Wright)*

A "footway" in the mature landscape of Radburn, New Jersey.

Thus was born a model version of the North American cul-de-sac. In the 1950s Stein wrote retrospectively about the scheme, which was only partially built because of the Great Depression:

> "The Radburn Idea," to answer the enigma "How to live with the auto," or, if you will, "How to live in spite of it," met these difficulties [of the menace of the automobile] with a radical revision of relation of houses, roads, paths, gardens, parks, blocks, and local neighborhoods.[16]

The mature landscape of Radburn today is delightful. However, later developers of residential subdivisions adopted Radburn's cost-saving and convenient dendritic street layouts while eliminating the connecting footways and shared parks. Often, they did not even provide sidewalks. Social activity between neighbors was decanted back into the street.

Another decentralization visionary who grappled with the implications of widespread adoption of the motor car was Frank Lloyd Wright. His Emersonian and Jeffersonian notions for what he called "Broadacre City" were refined and revisited over decades, from the 1930s to his death in 1959, though never implemented. The settlement pattern

proposition of Broadacres was to create a "new freedom for living in America" that would "automatically end unemployment and all its evils" by eliminating the political "mobocracy" of cities and towns and re-ruralizing the populace into minimum 4-acre agricultural plots for independent nuclear family homesteads, Wright claimed,

> All common interests take place in a simple coordination wherein all are employed: *little* farms, *little* homes for industry, *little* factories, *little* schools, a *little* university going to the people by way of their interest in the ground, *little* laboratories on their own ground for professional men.[17]

Never one to be shy or self-effacing, he set out to reconceive the basic land unit of the agricultural acre too, "improving" it into a broad proportion of 165 by 264 feet, replacing the conventional 66- by 660-foot acre that undergirds the U.S. Public Land Survey system as established in 1784. Residents would navigate the resulting pattern of very low-density, dispersed development in streamlined cars of Wright's own unique design, traveling at high speeds on extensive, grade-separated, multilevel freeways and in helicopter taxis providing door-to-door service.

Broadacre City, USA. Architectural model, 1934–1935. Wood. Frank
Lloyd Wright. Wright's anti-urban vision for the United States ("Usonia")
relied on a decentralized, locally provisioned settlement concept, blan-
keted across a midwestern landscape. Who was to lead and manage
Broadacre City? Not politicians or bureaucrats, but an architect.

In conventional subdivisions of recent vintage we can
experience the apotheosis of these varied early twentieth-
century visions for urban decentralization, as farm field,
forest, hillside, and desert landscapes were converted to
a seemingly endless dendritic pattern of roads lined with
detached dwellings, garage doors up front and center.
Although it is sobering to contemplate how visionary ideals
can so easily be watered down and diminished as they
propagate through the marketplace, we may still wonder, is
there merit in revisiting these schemes?

In the summer of 2011 curator Barry Bergdoll at
the Museum of Modern Art in New York undertook
the speculative project "Foreclosed: Rehousing
the American Dream." Five architect-led, interdisciplinary teams developed visionary schemes

for rethinking housing in suburbs in the wake of
the foreclosure crisis, in response to a hypoth-
esis proposed by architect and historian Reinhold
Martin, written in the form of a Socratic screen-
play challenging the roles and responsibilities of
the public sector in property markets. The challenge to the designers: "Change the dream and you
change the city."[18]

Two of the projects in particular resonate with
the historical paradigms under discussion here.
Nature-City, the Keizer, Oregon project designed
by a team led by Amale Andraos and Dan Wood of
WORKac, explicitly evokes the promise of Howard's
Garden City, to live symbiotically with nature, but
compresses it into higher-density form, inte-
grating ecological infrastructure. For example,

Nature-City project for Keizer, Oregon. Rendering and architectural model, 2011. WORKac. A vast raised compost mound for energy production from biogas is a central feature of this visionary contribution to the Museum of Modern Art's "Foreclosed: Rehousing the American Dream" show and book.

"Curbstoners" subdivided agricultural land and sold lots at roadside stands. Buyers built their own houses in working-class suburbs on the outskirts of Detroit, Michigan, 1941. John Vachon.

waste is literally compressed into a huge central compost mound topped with pools and housing that provides biogas to help fuel the settlement. The Garden in the Machine, led by Studio Gang Architects and sited in the working-class, Hispanic inner-Chicago suburb of Cicero, Illinois, inverts the pastoral paradigm of Leo Marx's classic thesis on nineteenth-century American culture by suggesting a densely diverse, flexible, and economically productive vision of an immigrant, working-class garden suburb. The model looks like a vertically stacked Broadacre City, full of democratic possibilities.

The work at the Museum of Modern Art was productively informed by the strategies and tactics articulated in the following chapters and explored in the Build a Better Burb competition schemes. What kinds of visions are useful to us now? How can and should new visions be disseminated, within architecture and urban design discourse and to the public at large? What are the advantages of working within existing systems, rather than challenging them from an outside critical position? What roles can cultural institutions play? Are there risks of a counterproductive backlash against a perceived elite?

Building and Selling the Dream

But there has been also the *American* dream, that dream of a land in which life should be better and richer and fuller for every man, with opportunity for each according to his ability or achievement.
– James Truslow Adams, *Epic of America* (1931)

In his popular history Adams distilled ideas that linked freedom and democracy, as well as the bountiful resources of the North American continent, to opportunities for each to attain success and prosperity. But achieving the American dream soon became almost inextricably linked with living in a detached house in suburbia, where land subdividers, homebuilders, and real estate agents kept themselves busy and profitable *building and selling the dream*.

Although home ownership, typically in a suburb, came over time to be a potent cultural marker denoting middle-class status, more so than income or profession, it is important to recognize that suburbs are not, and never were, as homogeneously white and middle class as many tend to imagine them. Some of the most persistent suburban stereotypes in the United States have their roots in marketing and lobbying campaigns of groups such as the National Association of Real Estate Brokers, who were explicitly in the business of profitably selling the dream.[19]

Photographer John Vachon, on assignment for the U.S. government, captured dozens of images in the early 1940s of self-built working-class housing on the outskirts of

– Working-class, self-built suburbs   – Federal Housing Administration
– Racially restrictive deeds and covenants   – Home Owners' Loan Corporation
– National Association of Real Estate Brokers   – Redlining

The Federal Housing Administration required developers of a new white subdivision to build a half-mile-long concrete wall to separate it from an existing black neighborhood. These poignant images attest to the existence of African American suburbs, countering persistent stereotypes. Detroit, Michigan, 1941. John Vachon.

Detroit. The African American neighborhood of Eight-Mile Wyoming, straddling the city's border, was segregated from an adjacent subdivision, restricted to whites, by a tall concrete wall. Officials from the Federal Housing Administration (FHA) insisted that the developer build the wall to segregate the neighborhoods before they would provide insurance for the new subdivision.[20]

The roots of structural racism in suburbia extend back to racially restrictive private deeds, as at the elite Country Club District in Kansas City, Missouri, developed by J. C. Nichols from 1906 to 1950. Then there are the infamous federally sanctioned Home Owners' Loan Corporation maps that led indirectly to the discriminatory private mortgage lending practice known as redlining, in reference to the districts marked red or "Fourth Grade" on these maps. Private loans became very difficult to obtain in these neighborhoods, once they were marked. The legacy of this shameful history persists today in predatory lending practices and racial steering.[21]

Not until 1950 did the FHA cease insuring projects with racially restrictive covenants. That same year, a case in the Canadian Supreme Court, concerning the right of a Jew to purchase resort property, had the effect of invalidating racially restrictive covenants.

The 2008 presidential election of Barack Obama shattered the old dichotomous model of Democratic cities and Republican suburbs, and recent demographic and geographic research supports a new, more complex model of metropolitan areas as a mosaic. This new model, described by Bernadette Hanlon, John Rennie Short, and Thomas J. Vicino in *Cities and Suburbs: New Metropolitan Realities in the US*, posits areas of affluence and need, of homogeneity and diversity, of growth and decline throughout metropolitan areas in ways that cannot be neatly categorized.[22]

In his introduction to the edited volume *Social Justice in Diverse Suburbs*, sociologist Christopher Niedt describes ongoing class and race exclusion but also suggests inroads are being made in attaining and sustaining social justice in these communities. One example, which I describe in Niedt's book, concerns activism at Downtown Silver Spring, Maryland to assert free speech rights on the street and sidewalks of a lifestyle center shopping mall developed with public subsidy.[23]

What is the legacy of structural racism in North American suburbs? How do we best measure, and nurture, true metropolitan diversity? How do we provide access to opportunity and support an equitable "right to the suburb"?

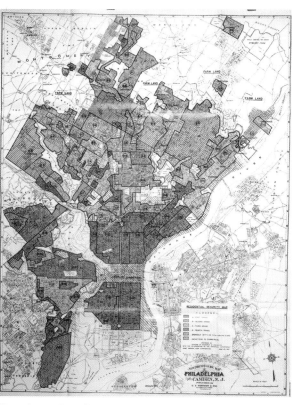

Home Owners Loan Corporation Residential Security Map for
Philadelphia, Pennsylvania, 1937. The areas in red are marked "D"
and "Fourth Grade," whereas most suburban areas are graded "First"
(green) and "Second" (blue). Blatantly racist criteria were used in the
assessments. Although these maps were meant to identify areas in
need of government loan assistance, they soon found their way into the
hands of private bankers, who refused to lend in "redlined" areas.

Timeline:

Buying and Selling the American Dream

1906

Construction of Country
Club District in Kansas City,
Missouri, begins. J.C. Nichols
(1880–1950) cited as an early
"community builder"

CC&Rs – Covenants, conditions
and restrictions developed as
planning tool by J.C. Nichols

1908

NAREB – National Assoc. of
Real Estate Boards founded, J.C.
Nichols was a prominent member

1910s

Private deed restrictions are
common in North America

1922

First model building code
adopted

1924 and 1928

Model zoning laws, adopted ver-
batim by many state legislatures

1929

Herbert Hoover (R) elected
president: 1929–1933

Stock Market Crash, beginning of
the Great Depression

1926

U.S. Supreme Court upholds
zoning in *Euclid v. Ambler*

1931

President Hoover's Conference
on Home Building and Home
Ownership, spurs transition from
"subdividing" to "homebuilding"
as a major economic sector

1933

Franklin D. Roosevelt elected
president (D): 1933–1945,
Architect of the "New Deal"

HOLC – Home Owners Loan
Corporation: "New Deal"
program (1933–1951) founded,
intended to prevent foreclosure

1934

National Housing Act established
the FHA, to help boost employment in the housing sector

FHA – Federal Housing
Administration: Established to
insure home mortgages; intended
to stimulate construction jobs

Homer Hoyt, housing economist,
joins the FHA. Develops real
estate theories about factors
leading to neighborhood "deterio-
ration," codified in HOLC maps

1936

Urban Land Institute (ULI), spin-
off of NAREB, is founded by J.C.
Nichols

1948

U.S. Supreme Court decision
Shelley v. Kraemer makes
racially restrictive covenants
unenforceable

1950

Canadian Supreme Court decision in *Noble and Wolf v. Alley*
finds that racially restrictive
covenants do not "run with the
land" in resale agreements

FHA ceases insuring projects
with racially restrictive covenants

1964

Herbert Hoover dies

1968

Fair Housing Act makes the
discriminatory practice of "redlining" illegal

2007

Collapse of U.S. subprime mortgage market, which had fueled
a sustained suburban housing
boom, precipitates 2007–2012
global financial crisis

"I bought the lawn in six-foot rolls. It's easy to handle. I prepared the ground and my wife and son helped roll out the grass. In one day you have a front yard." 1973. Bill Owens.

Cul-de-Sac Paradigm

Now we come to the *cul-de-sac paradigm*, comprising the period of mass suburbanization resulting in many thousands of new subdivisions and planned suburban communities. Most in the United States were built in strict conformance with FHA standards, in response to the pent-up demand for new dwellings in the wake of the double whammy of the Great Depression and World War II. In the housing boom of 1944–1965, a remarkable twenty-six million new nonfarm homes were built in the United States, mostly in suburbs, and mostly by a small coterie of large homebuilders.[24] Significantly, the groundwork prepared by the would-be builders and dream sellers ensured that these homes were largely detached and located in suburbs. The federal government bolstered suburban home ownership by providing for mortgages with little or no down payment through the G.I. Bill (with payments of less than $60 a month at Levittown, New York).

Park Forest, outside Chicago, occupied beginning in 1948, was an iconic example of a postwar planned community, memorialized in the mid-1950s as the preferred dormitory of William H. Whyte's "organization man" and his family.[25] Amid the hypersocial kaffeeklatsches, Newcomers' Club dinners, and family night around television's "window on the world," a new conformist social norm was solidified for white, middle-class postwar men and women, Whyte contended. Park Forest was also notable for its master plan, by well-known planner Elbert Peets. It was originally conceived as a garden city suburb, with Radburn-type culs-de-sac around shared greens and a central shopping plaza modeled on the classical agora ideal, surrounded by low-rise garden apartment courts. Initial plans showed a rail spur to a train station at the center. In the end, however, Park Forest was reconceived to conform to the standards the FHA codified, inhibiting flexibility or variation. The master plan was reconfigured to feature detached houses on curved roads without shared greens, aping the wildly successful scheme concurrently in construction at Levittown, New York. The Park Forest Plaza, though progressive in design, never got its train station.[26]

– *Mass-produced postwar housing: Lakewood,*
  Levittown, Park Forest
– *William H. Whyte's "organization man"*

– *Window on the world of television*
– *Rise of the environmental movement*
– *Second-wave feminism*

Woman holding coffee pot standing next to group of women neighbors seated in lawn chairs, Park Forest, Illinois, 1954. Bob Sandberg for *Look* magazine. Kaffeeklatsch gatherings, indoors and out, were a central feature of women's social life in the era of postwar mass suburbanization.

The developers of Lakewood, California hired a photographer to document different phases of the subdivision's construction from his Cessna airplane. 1950. William Garnett.

Another iconic postwar planned subdivision was Lakewood, near Los Angeles, begun in 1950, where large-scale production builders took advantage (criminally, it was later alleged) of federal loan programs to efficiently transform large tracts of agricultural land into a massive residential subdivision of wood-framed small houses, seemingly overnight. The awesomely stark photographs by William Garnett, resembling nothing less than a very large-scale production line, offer testimony to the rapidity of the construction process. *Holy Land*, a lyrical memoir by writer and Lakewood city planner D. J. Waldie, movingly attests to the bittersweet experiences of life and faith in such communities, whether built with limited-access gridded streets like Lakewood or filled with the "loop and lollipop" pattern of dead ends that soon became the suburban subdivision norm. Waldie, a baby boomer who still lives in the house he grew up in, writes,

> You leave the space between the houses uncrossed.
> You rarely go across the street, which is forty feet wide.
> You are grateful for the distance. It is as if each house on your block stood on its own enchanted island, fifty feet wide by one hundred feet long.
>
> People come and go from it, your parents mostly and your friends. Your parents arrive like pilgrims.

> But the island is remote. You occasionally hear the sounds of anger. You almost never hear the sounds of love.
>
> You hear, always at night, the shifting of the uprights, the sagging of ceiling joists, and the unpredictable ticking of the gas heater. [27]

The cultural backlash to the postwar tract suburbs was almost immediate. Singer Malvina Reynolds mocked the "ticky tacky" houses of Daly City, California and countless other places in her popular 1962 folk song "Little Boxes," later recorded by Pete Seeger. The song evokes iconic bird's-eye photos of postwar subdivisions such as Garnett's of Lakewood. A decade later, photographer Bill Owens conveyed a more empathic, ground-up, "worm's-eye" view of social life in these subdivisions.[28] Owens matter-of-factly quotes the man of the family laying sod, his neighbors in Livermore, California, in the caption to one of his photos: "I bought the lawn in six-foot rolls. It's easy to handle…. In one day you have a front yard." Well, why not?

However, the lawns were not benign. The spawn of this period includes the rise of environmentalism in response to the rise of the "suburban–industrial complex," as documented by environmental historian Adam Rome in *The Bulldozer in the Countryside*, another wordplay on the machine in the garden.[29] Suburbanites were aghast at

Untitled, 1973, Bill Owens.

Vacant strip mall in Colorado Springs, Colorado, 2011.

pollution in rivers and lakes that was traced to their own backyards. Nondegradable detergents from faulty septic tanks and cesspools turned up as frothy tap water, dubbed "white beer" by residents moved by frustration and fear to become environmental activists.[30] Second-wave feminism also emerged in this period, as many of those kaffee-klatsching housewives became deeply disillusioned with their great good fortune.[31] But the building of bedroom subdivisions continued apace.

In her astute essay "How Hell Moved from the City to the Suburbs," historian Becky Nicolaides writes perceptively about the elitism of urbanist critics of postwar suburbia — Lewis Mumford, Jane Jacobs, and William H. Whyte — who, embracing to some degree concepts of environmental determinism, were moved to condemn postwar suburbanites along with their choice of settlement form. In highly influential books these writers shifted the locus on an urban critique that had formerly targeted cities as places of anomie and social dysfunction. "Hell, it seemed, was moving from the cities to the suburbs — like everyone else."[32]

Although there was, and is, much to interrogate about the environmental, economic, racial, gendered, and public health impacts of the bedroom suburb norm that spread in popularity in the postwar period and has persisted in various forms to the present, it is important to be wary of critiques that slip into blanket, stereotypical condemnations.

Why are mid- and late twentieth-century dystopian cultural tropes in film and television about suburbs, suburbanites, and the middle class so persistent, especially in popular culture? Do these stereotypes impede the development of new narratives of change and transformation for a more resilient future for suburbia? If so, how might they be successfully reframed?

Sprawl Paradigm

The late twentieth century saw an explosion of nonresidential development in suburbs, as office jobs and retail decanted out of center cities into an expanded metropolitan landscape. This is the *sprawl paradigm*. The five components of sprawl, identified by new urbanists Andrés Duany, Elizabeth Plater-Zyberk, and Jeff Speck in their cri de coeur *Suburban Nation*, are housing subdivisions or pods for living; malls, strip centers, and big boxes for shopping; office "parks" for working; civic institutions such as town halls, churches, and schools on isolated campuses; and, finally, miles and miles of roadways.[33]

Metropolitan geography morphed as functions that had once been concentrated in center cities increasingly relocated to peripheral areas, serviced by infrastructure for automobiles and trucks. Vast, unplanned agglomerations, or "edge cities," of office parks and shopping malls sprung

— Problems of defining sprawl
— Edge and edgeless cities
— Very-low-density exurban development
— Gated communities
— Onset of the Great Recession

The happy just-married couple enjoy a ride at Camp Snoopy theme park in the Mall of America, Bloomington, Minnesota, 1994. © Martin Parr/ Magnum Photos.

up like mushrooms at interstate highway interchanges. "Edgeless cities" and "boomburgs" soon followed.[34]

Supersized regional shopping malls with trade areas of 25 miles (40 kilometers), or larger if an international airport was nearby, were built as all-in-one destinations, with hotels, themed entertainment components complete with rides, and millions of square feet of gross leasable area. The 1992 Mall of America in Bloomington, Minnesota was arguably the last of its breed in North America, unless the troubled American Dream Meadowlands project in New Jersey (formerly Meadowlands Xanadu) is opened. Unfortunately, developers in China have continued the folly; the vast New South China Mall opened with fanfare in 2006, hubristically claiming the title of the world's largest shopping center. But by 2011 it was only 2 percent leased, the vast atriums gathering dust, the Venetian canal attraction unused.

In *Edge City: Life on the New Frontier*, journalist Joel Garreau nevertheless reassured readers that Americans were "pretty smart cookies" and that, somehow, we would seek and find order in these hyperprivatized non-place places.[35] Will he eventually be proven right? The dramatic transformations afoot in Tysons Corner, the über–edge city near Dulles Airport in Virginia, suggest a tentative "yes."[36] But there is so much more to be done to stave off the environmental devastation set in motion by the accumulated effects of conventional land use and development practices of the late twentieth century.

While these office and retail agglomerations were growing, common interest communities proliferated. Many such communities are gated off from their surroundings, allowable because the streets are private, not public. Many of these gated communities popped up in exurban locations, out on the metropolitan fringes, "where once there were greenfields." The exclusionary nature of manned security gates, regardless of whether they actually increase safety and inhibit crime, contributes to a culture of fear and diminishes both social capital and the public realm. Gating, conspicuous consumption, and McMansioning all contribute to suburban social anxiety, as the bar for achieving and maintaining middle-class status appears to rise.[37]

So where are we now? Are we sprawled out, or is the current recession just a pause in an inexorable process?

As we consider the ongoing impacts of global economic crisis that began in 2007 with the U.S. mortgage securities market implosion, it is sobering to consider the millions of entitled but not-yet-built house lots and commercially zoned parcels that exist throughout the United States in premature and obsolete subdivisions, especially in the western and southern regions of the country. A premature subdivision occurs when a landowner divides a parcel of land into lots for sale far in advance of the market for those lots, usually to increase the land's appraised value. Pinal County in Arizona has 600,000 of such lots alone, enough to accommodate a growth rate of 6 percent for 28 years. Premature subdivisions are having the stultifying effect of locking in obsolete assumptions about the form future growth will take, namely, suburban residential subdivisions-as-usual, served with large strip malls, big box stores, office parks, and little or no mass transit.[38]

Many persist in arguing that sprawl is simply what "the market" wants and that it will always be with us.[39] Perhaps, up to a point. Recent research into real estate markets suggests a new direction, a smart turn toward "walkable urbanism" and away from "driveable suburbanism," to use Christopher Leinberger's terms from his optimistic primer *The Option of Urbanism*. His analysis suggests that people are increasingly willing to pay a premium for locations near mass transit. He argues that actions must be taken to preserve affordability in these sites. In *Reshaping Metropolitan America* Arthur C. Nelson similarly suggests that the United States is vastly oversupplied with detached houses on large lots, and future markets will consist of households demanding a more diverse set of settlement choices.[40]

These studies and others provide designers and planners with significant food for thought. How do we effectively influence patterns of desire and other cultural aspirations — for new cars, for larger dwellings, for air conditioning, for more and more *stuff* — here in North America and elsewhere around the globe? How can we best leverage the lessons of the history of suburbanization, and its discontents, to help shape a better future?

Notes

1. Ellen Dunham-Jones and June Williamson, *Retrofitting Suburbia: Urban Design Solutions for Redesigning Suburbs*, updated edition (Hoboken, NJ: Wiley, 2011), xxvi–xxviii. See also Kiril Stanilov and Brenda Case Scheer, eds., *Suburban Form: An International Perspective* (New York: Routledge, 2004).

2. Number for United States from U.S. 2010 Census: http://2010.census.gov/2010census/. For Canada, Canada 2011 Census: http://www.statcan.gc.ca.

3. Laura Carstensen, "A Hopeful Future," in Henry Cisneros, Margaret Dyer-Chamberlain, and Jane Hickie, eds., *Independent for Life: Homes and Neighborhoods for an Aging America* (Austin: University of Texas Press, 2012), 21–31.

4. Andrew Jackson Downing, *Cottage Residences: or, A Series of Designs for Rural Cottages and Adapted to North America* (1842; New York: Dover, 1981) and *The Architecture of Country Houses* (New York: D. Appleton, 1850). Catharine Beecher, *A Treatise on Domestic Economy* (New York, 1847) and Catharine Beecher and Harriet Beecher Stowe, *The American Women's Home* (1869; Hartford, CT: Stowe–Day Foundation, 1987).

5. Dolores Hayden, *The Grand Domestic Revolution* (Cambridge, MA: MIT Press, 1981), 54–63.

6. Leo Marx, *The Machine in the Garden: Technology and the Pastoral Ideal in America* (Oxford, England: Oxford University Press, 1964).

7. Ibid., 13–14.

8. Frederick Law Olmsted, "Preliminary Report upon the Proposed Suburban Village at Riverside near Chicago," reprinted in *Landscape Architecture* 21 (July 1931):262.

9. See Robert Fishman, *Bourgeois Utopias: The Rise and Fall of Suburbia* (New York: Basic Books, 1987), for a more thorough history of the cultural ideology of Anglo-American suburbs.

10. Dolores Hayden, "What Would a Non-Sexist City Be Like? Speculations on Housing, Urban Design, and Human Work," in Catharine R. Stimpson et al., eds., *Women and the American City* (Chicago: University of Chicago Press, 1981), 167–84.

11. Peter G. Rowe, *Making a Middle Landscape* (Cambridge, MA: MIT Press, 1991).

12. Henry C. Binford, *The First Suburbs: Residential Communities on the Boston Periphery, 1815–1860* (Chicago: University of Chicago Press, 1985). Kenneth T. Jackson, *Crabgrass Frontier: The Suburbanization of the United States* (New York: Oxford University Press, 1985), 103–15.

13. Patrick M. Condon, *Seven Rules for Sustainable Communities: Design Strategies for the Post-Carbon World* (Washington, DC: Island Press, 2010), 24–25.

14. Ibid., 34–38.

15. Ebenezer Howard, *Garden Cities of To-Morrow* (London: Swan Sonnenschein, 1902).

16. Clarence S. Stein, *Toward New Towns for America* (New York: Reinhold, 1957), 37–73.

17. Frank Lloyd Wright, "Broadacre City: A New Community Plan," *Architectural Record* (1935).

18. Barry Bergdoll and Reinhold Martin, *Foreclosed: Rehousing the American Dream* (New York: Museum of Modern Art, 2012).

19. Dolores Hayden, chapter 6, "Mail-Order and Self-Built Suburbs," *Building Suburbia: Green Fields and Urban Growth, 1820–2000* (New York: Pantheon, 2003), 97–127.

20. For more on African American suburbanization, see Andrew Wiese, *Places of Their Own: African American Suburbanization in the Twentieth Century* (Chicago: University of Chicago Press, 2005).

21. Jackson, *Crabgrass Frontier*, 190–218. For more recent treatment of the topic, see Amy Hillier, "Redlining and the Home Owners' Loan Corporation," *Journal of Urban History* 29:4(2003):394–420.

22. Bernadette Hanlon, John Rennie Short, and Thomas J. Vicino, *Cities and Suburbs: New Metropolitan Realities in the US* (New York: Routledge, 2010).

23. Christopher Niedt, ed., *Social Justice and the Diverse Suburb* (Philadelphia: Temple University Press, 2013).

24. Becky M. Nicolaides and Andrew Wiese, eds., *The Suburb Reader* (New York: Routledge, 2006), 257–58.

25. William H. Whyte, Jr., *The Organization Man* (New York: Simon & Schuster, 1956).

26. For a good summary of Park Forest and other postwar communities, see Dolores Hayden, chapter 7, "Sitcom Suburbs," in *Building Suburbia: Green Fields and Urban Growth, 1820–2000* (New York: Pantheon, 2003), 128–53. For a detailed study, see Gregory C. Randall, *America's Original GI Town: Park Forest, Illinois* (Baltimore, MD: Johns Hopkins University Press, 2000).

27. D. J. Waldie, *Holy Land: A Suburban Memoir* (New York: W.W. Norton, 1996), 12–13.

28. Bill Owens, *Suburbia* (San Francisco: Straight Arrow Books, 1973).

29. Adam Rome, *The Bulldozer in the Countryside: Suburban Sprawl and the Rise of American Environmentalism* (New York: Cambridge University Press, 2001).

30. Ibid., 103–14.

31. Betty Friedan, *The Feminine Mystique* (New York: W.W. Norton, 1963).

32. Becky Nicolaides, "How Hell Moved from the City to the Suburbs," in Kevin M. Kruse and Thomas J. Sugrue, eds., *The New Suburban History* (Chicago: University of Chicago Press, 2006), 80–98.

33. Andrés Duany, Elizabeth Plater-Zyberk, and Jeff Speck, *Suburban Nation: The Rise of Sprawl and the Decline of the American Dream* (New York: North Point Press, 2000), 5–7.

34. See Robert Lang, *Edgeless Cities: Exploring the Elusive Metropolis* (Washington, DC: Brookings Institution Press, 2003), and Robert B. Lang and Jennifer LeFurgy, *Boomburbs: The Rise of America's Accidental Cities* (Washington, DC: Brookings Institution Press, 2007).

35. Joel Garreau, *Edge City: Life on the New Frontier* (New York: Doubleday, 1991).

36. For more on the plans for Tysons Corner, see the Fairfax County, Virginia website "Transforming Tysons": http://www.fairfaxcounty.gov/tysons/.

37. On gating, see Setha Low, *Behind the Gates: Life, Security, and the Pursuit of Happiness in Fortress America* (New York: Routledge, 2003). On middle-class anxiety, see Rachel Heiman, "Gate Expectations: Discursive Displacement of the 'Old Middle Class' in an American Suburb," in Rachel Heiman, Carla Freeman, and Mark Liechty, eds., *The Global Middle Classes: Theorizing through Ethnography* (Sante Fe, NM: SAR Press, 2012).

38. Donald Elliott, "Premature Subdivisions and What to Do about Them," Lincoln Institute of Land Policy Working Paper (2010).

39. The most scholarly example, perhaps, is Robert Bruegmann, *Sprawl: A Compact History* (Chicago: University of Chicago Press, 2005).

40. Christopher B. Leinberger, *The Option of Urbanism: Investing in a New American Dream* (Washington, DC: Island Press, 2007). Arthur C. Nelson, *Reshaping Metropolitan America: Development Trends and Opportunities to 2030* (Washington, DC: Island Press, 2013).

A lone security guard watches over one of the ghostly
courts at the New South China Mall in Dongguan,
opened in 2005. Matthew Niederhauser/INSTITUTE.

Design Culture Responds to Sprawl:

1960s to 2010s

The six historical paradigms of suburbanization – the pastoral paradigm, the streetcar suburb paradigm, the visionary schemes paradigm, the paradigm for building and selling the dream, the postwar cul-de-sac paradigm, and the most recent paradigm of rapacious sprawl – figure heavily in the cultural imagination of North America and throughout the globe and continue to exert power-ful forces on developers, planners, policy makers, and ordinary citizens. How has the architectural and urban design discourse responded to the sprawling suburban landscape, especially in the last half century, as mass suburbanization dramatically reshaped settlement patterns across the continent? How did design culture respond to the suburbanization trends that profoundly informed daily lived experience: the dwellings we lived in; the vehicles we owned and drove to work, to shopping malls, and to school; the entertainments we enjoyed, at the multiplex theater or on our couches; the exercise we did or did not get; the energy and resources we consumed; the social relationships we formed?

Starting in the 1960s, architects commenced a criti-cal engagement with the tremendously fast-growing and mutating suburban territory. In this chapter I trace selected protagonists in architecture and urban design discourse up to those working today on imagining and designing new suburban futures. These discursive debates have staked out positions that have affected – sometimes subtly, sometimes in more profound ways – suburban form in North America and elsewhere through the dissemination of designers' images and writings.

1960s–1970s: The Vernacular and the Ordinary

At the same time that influential urban writers Jane Jacobs, Lewis Mumford, and William H. Whyte were collectively declaring that hell had moved to the suburbs, some architects were beginning to question this blanket con-demnation, applied both to mass culture suburbia and to middle-class suburbanites. Certainly there was sufficient cause for concern and consternation from these critics, as they observed populations draining away in significant numbers from older urban neighborhoods in New York and many other cities. But did they go too far?

Architect Charles W. Moore, influenced by scholars of vernacular buildings and landscapes such as J. B. Jackson, articulated a new design appreciation for the phenomeno-logical experience of place in projects both "high" and "low." Moore's projects include the exclusive timber-framed and wood-clad Sea Ranch condominium (1965) on the rugged northern California coast and low-income housing projects such as the wood-shingled Whitman Housing (1974) in Huntington, Long Island, near the Walt Whitman Mall.[1]

In the late 1960s Robert Venturi and Denise Scott Brown were invited by Moore, then dean of the Yale University School of Architecture, to offer research-based architecture studios, one titled "Learning from Las Vegas, or Form Analysis as Design Research" and the other, "Learning from Levittown, or Remedial Housing for Architects." The traveling studios were novel for the time, conceived with thumbed noses at prevailing modernist

Tableau of split-level house and yard, from 1976 exhibition "Sign of Life: Symbols in the American City," designed by Venturi, Scott Brown and Associates, Inc.

pedagogy and consciously inspired by Pop art. Venturi, Scott Brown, and their collaborator Steven Izenour wrote,

> Modern architects, who can embrace vernacular architecture remote in place or time, can contemptuously reject the current vernacular of the United States, that is, the merchant builders' vernacular of Levittown and the commercial vernacular of Route 66.... They understand the symbolism of Levittown and do not like it, nor are they prepared to suspend judgment on it in order to learn and, by learning, to make subsequent judgment more sensitive.[2]

The research ideas of the Yale studios were reprised and developed for the 1976 exhibit "Signs of Life: Symbols in the American City" at the Smithsonian Institution's

Renwick Gallery in Washington, D.C. Scott Brown and her associates, decoding the semiotic meanings of detached houses in bedroom suburbs of the "middle-middle class," tagged saltbox houses with speech balloons and thought bubbles suggesting the historical aspirations signified by a short segment of white-painted split-rail fence, coach lanterns, or a miniature pediment over the front door.[3]

Also in 1976, Robert A. M. Stern, who as a young architect had aligned himself against the early Corbu-influenced "Whites" (Eisenman, Graves, Gwathmey, Hejduk, and Meier) and with the "Grays" (including Moore, Venturi and Scott Brown, and Jaquelin Robertson), was included in the inaugural architecture exhibit at the Venice Biennale. Inspired by the Philadelphia railroad suburb of Chestnut Hill, he designed the hypothetical "Subway Suburb" project. He explains that the project "called for the introduction

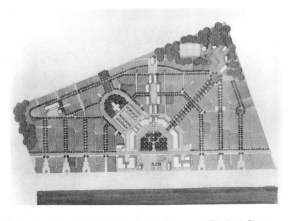

Town plan of Seaside, Florida by Andrés Duany and Elizabeth Plater-Zyberk. Construction of the new–old beach resort town began in 1981.

"Stairway to Heaven" townhouse on Seaside's Ruskin Place, designed in a modernist idiom by architect Alexander Gorlin. The Seaside code prescribes materials and some formal massing properties but not style.

of the garden suburb type into those areas of the central cities where the prevailing mode of redevelopment – the disconnected vertical garden cities of towers in the park – had clearly failed."[4] Provocatively, he sited the proposal in the Brooklyn neighborhood of Brownsville, one of the areas of New York City most profoundly devastated at that time with poverty, crime, white flight, disinvestment, and the impacts of urban renewal policies. A few years later, in 1981, Stern and co-author John Massengale presented "The Anglo-American Suburb," a meticulously researched exhibit at the Cooper-Hewitt Museum, published as an *AD Profile* monograph, that grandly reintroduced the history of planned pastoral and garden suburbs, including Olmsted's Riverside, Stein and Wright's Sunnyside Gardens, Radburn, and many others.[5]

The professional and academic interest in vernacular architectures and traditional forms of urbanism, explored under the rubric of postmodernism, was set in opposition to the products of orthodox modernism in design: towers-in-the-park housing, mass-produced little boxes on hillsides, and commercial and institutional buildings designed as icons. What did this debate mean for the building, or rebuilding, of actual suburbs?

1980s: Urbanism Revivals

The construction of Seaside, a startlingly new–old resort town built on 80 oceanfront acres on the Florida pan-handle, inspired by the existing local vernacular of wood beach cottages with metal roofs, commenced in the early

1980s. Seaside was developed by Robert Davis to a radial master plan created by young architects Andrés Duany and Elizabeth Plater-Zyberk, who split from their partnership in the Miami firm Arquitectonica and struck out on their own during the course of the project. They sought input for the plan from neotraditionalist provocateur Leon Krier, who came to Florida, participated in a design charrette, and sharply reshaped the final master plan.[6]

The influential new precedent of Seaside, and projects of others similarly interested in selectively exploring the merits of pre–World War II urban development patterns, shifted the discourse on new market-rate housing in North America toward a reconsideration of urban form and neighborhood design. This shift rendered the choices for architects and landscape architects who wanted to engage with the design of new communities in suburban settings in a fresh light. This realm had not been entirely ceded to large production homebuilders, it turned out. Although many saw sepia-toned nostalgia lacking in urban grit in Seaside's crushed-shell streets and white wooden fences, Seaside did offer a stark rebuke to conventional subdivision practice. The houses were not cookie-cutter, and the architectural code, though restricting materials, offered a great deal of design flexibility. In the event, though, many residents chose neotraditional designs for their dwellings.

Seaside also offered a rebuke to the practice of building high-rise beachside condominiums, architect-designed developments that threatened protective dunes, relied heavily on air conditioning, and blocked views for

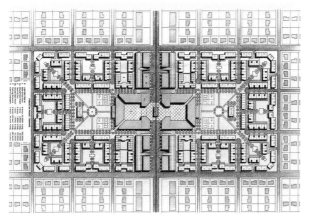

Diagram published in the 1990s of a "pedestrian pocket," by Peter Calthorpe, the beginnings of the planning concept of transit-oriented development, or TOD.

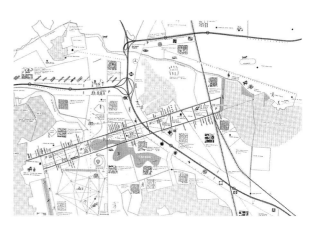

Drawing submitted by Rem Koolhaas and the Office for Metropolitan Architecture for a 1987 competition to master plan the Ville Nouvelle (New Town) of Melun-Sénart, outside Paris.

those further inland. Advocacy for traditional neighborhood developments as an alternative to conventional suburban developments became Duany and Plater-Zyberk's mission, and they found sizable market interest. However, conventional zoning codes, building and lot regulations, street standards, and developer's practices and pro formas stood in the way and had to be engaged and reformed, a complex, one might say radical, process that is still ongoing.[7]

A group of academic architects on the West Coast also began to critically reexamine suburban settlement patterns and to advocate for good urbanism as an essential component of ecologically sensitive, energy-efficient design. They began to argue that it was not sufficient to design passive solar, naturally ventilated buildings. Douglas Kelbaugh in Seattle invited Peter Calthorpe of San Francisco and others together to collaborate on concepts crystallized in the diagram of a 100-acre "pedestrian pocket" of walkability around a transit stop, a revival of the streetcar suburb paradigm combined with garden city planning, as a way to communicate their values. This diagram became the forerunner of the now-mainstream planning concept of transit-oriented development.[8]

Meanwhile, Rem Koolhaas and the Office for Metropolitan Architecture followed the phenomenal success in 1978 of *Delirious New York* with a provocative series of projects of the 1980s that were organized as "horizontal" or "vertical" in one classification, or "S, M, L, or XL" in another.[9] One of the horizontal, extra-large projects is the 1987 urban plan for the New Town of

Melun-Sénart, outside Paris, designed for a competition. The proposal was to inscribe onto the site a series of bandlike voids, shaped to resemble a Chinese ideogram, for preservation of existing historic village fabric and conservation of open space. The rest of the territory – the "interbands" – would be ceded over to islands of differentiated new development. This project, unrealized, seemed both a visionary attempt to reorder sprawl and a concession to the banal, generic quality of "the average-contemporary-everyday ugliness of current European-American-Japanese architecture."[10] Koolhaas asserted that the contrast between the empty and the new might produce a "sublime contrast," a position later dubbed "post urbanism" by Douglas Kelbaugh.[11]

1990s: Responses to the Decline of Public Space

By the early 1990s, with the rise of edge cities, attention had largely shifted from the residential suburban realm to the commercial. A full-throated critique arose, targeting the inauthenticity of the agglomerations of office buildings and shopping malls springing up around highway interchanges. The title of the hugely popular 1992 volume edited by architect and critic Michael Sorkin, *Variations on a Theme Park: The New American City and the End of Public Space*, said it all. Suburbanites were marooned in glitzed up, sanitized theme parks, insulated from messy, democratic confrontations with

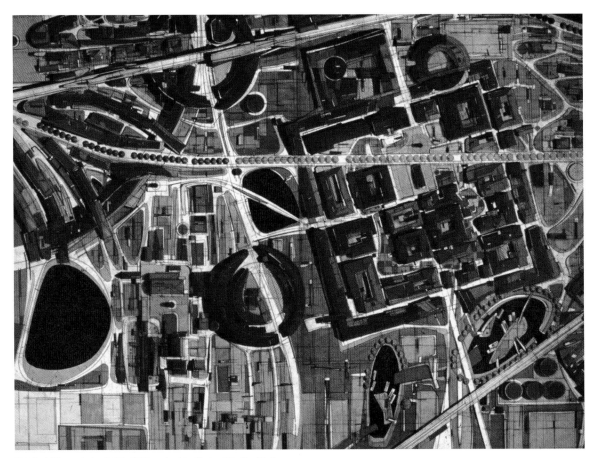

Detail of "Neurasia," a 1995–1996 project by Michael Sorkin Studio proposing an ecologically self-sufficient imaginary city located somewhere between Hong Kong and Hanoi.

social, economic, and environmental reality and divorced from the ecological impacts of their consumption.[12] Sorkin soon began a series of hypothetical projects, only slightly tongue-in-cheek, exploring a sustainable, car-free, walkable urbanism comprised of five-story walkup buildings layered with small-scale agriculture and energy production for self-sufficiency in aggregated settlement, a theme he has continued to pursue.

One essay in the volume, by historian Margaret Crawford, titled "The World in a Shopping Mall," drove home the message. The essay is focused primarily on the spectacle of the massive 5.2-million-square-foot West Edmonton Mall but also considers how cultural centers and museums had come to duplicate the layouts and formats of malls. "The world of the shopping mall – respecting no boundaries, no longer limited even by the imperative of consumption – has become the world," she wrote.[13]

A decade later it had become clear that the suburban shopping mall type that had transfixed the discourse of public space was actually entering the twilight of decline. The Congress for the New Urbanism, officially founded in 1993 by Duany and Plater-Zyberk along with Peter Calthorpe, Elizabeth Moule, Stefanos Polyzoides, and Dan Solomon, responded in 2001 with publication of *Greyfields into Goldfields*.[14] The study, authored primarily by Lee Sobel, documented dozens of examples of failed regional malls that had been successfully – read also as profitably – redeveloped. It was an eye-opening study, including the examples of Mizner Park in Boca Raton, Mashpee Commons on Cape Cod, Phalen Village Center in St. Paul, Eastgate Town Center in Tennessee, Belmar in Lakewood, Colorado, and many others. It demonstrated that the retrofitting of obsolete and disinvested commercial real estate, much of it in postwar suburbs, was possible.

Photorealistic perspective views rendered in the late 1990s for an edge city retrofit, used to promote the advantages of adopting a form-based overlay code developed by Dover, Kohl and Partners and Duany Plater-Zyberk & Company. Note the "before" and "after" condition of the man's necktie.

2000s: Between the Local and the Global

The Los Angeles Forum for Architecture and Urban Design sponsored the pioneering Dead Malls competition in 2002–2003. The brief of the open, two-part ideas competition was to envision the future of the shopping mall, just as increasing numbers of large regional malls in North America were heading toward dereliction and abandonment (although mall building was, and still is, on the upswing in eastern Europe, the Middle East, Latin America, and Asia). Competitors were asked to identify and research a mall in decline, anywhere in North America, in which to set their design proposal. Two of the winning schemes in the competition have proved particularly influential: Stoner Meek Architecture's "Pell Mall" and Interboro Partners' "In the Meantime, Life with Landbanking."

In "Pell Mall," Berkeley, California–based Stoner Meek presented a strategy of regreening and environmental repair, proposing the reengineering of wetlands and bird habitat at the Vallejo Plaza mall, on San Francisco Bay. The Brooklyn-based design collaborative of Interboro Partners, currently comprised of Tobias Amborst, Daniel D'Oca, and Georgeen Theodore, former students of Margaret Crawford, formed over the competition, which they recognized as an ideal vehicle for applying the ideas of everyday urbanism they had been absorbing in graduate school. "In the Meantime, Life with Landbanking," a scheme for Dutchess County Mall in Fishkill, New York, proposed a collection of inexpensive moves that could be added incrementally over time to support and enhance the many odd and mundane activities already happening there, leading to many possible futures. The roots of a fruitful but critical small-scale, bottom-up approach are found here.

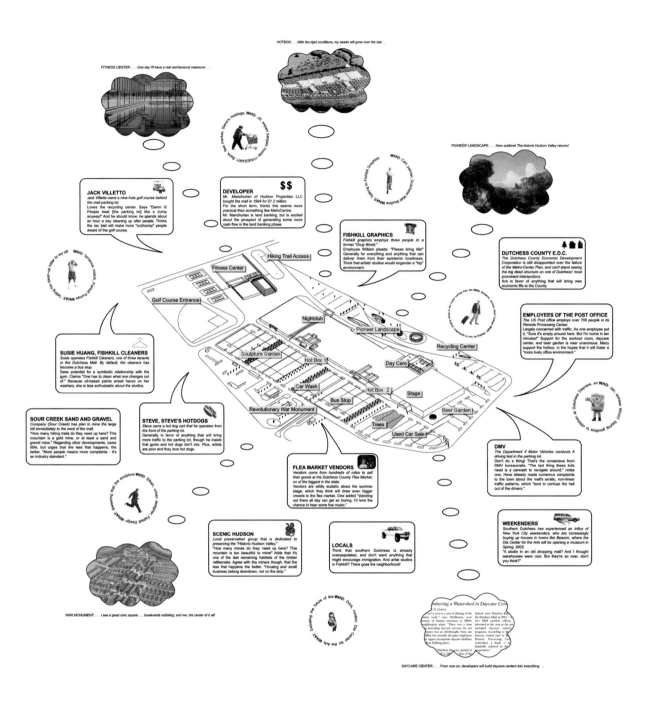

Drawing of "Life with Landbanking," a winning scheme by Interboro Partners for the 2002–2003 Dead Malls competition. The designers observed a plethora of small-scale, everyday activities and exchanges occurring at the seemingly abandoned property and proposed interventions to enhance them.

The adaptive design process elaborated by architect Paul Lukez in his 2007 book *Suburban Transformations*, applied hypothetically to the Burlington Mall in Massachusetts.

In 2007, Boston-based architect Paul Lukez published *Suburban Transformations*, introducing a method he called the "adaptive design process," for more organic, gradual transformation of large-scale, single-use sites into places with richer identity, informed by complex layers of mapping using geographic information systems and digital design tools. Case studies of the method range from three U.S. malls to peripheral sites in Amsterdam and Shenzhen. The global focus of this research reflects significant shifts that occurred in the world economy, making it impossible to examine development trends within neatly circumscribed national boundaries when the capital, and debt, behind urban development flows freely.[15]

Galina Tachieva, a partner in the Miami office of Duany Plater-Zyberk & Company and the designer behind many of the firm's innovative suburban retrofitting proposals, developed over many years for several clients, published the manifesto-type book *Sprawl Repair Manual* in 2010.[16] The book provides a set of steps for analyzing sprawling suburban sites at various scales, following New Urbanist tenets, from the metropolitan region to the neighborhood to the single lot and building. Her sights are not set on

functioning elite suburbs, or streetcar suburb fabric, but rather on postwar residential and commercial sprawl. The before-and-after graphics, consistently rendered in pencil and watercolor axonometric views, are very clear to read and convincing. Debates have arisen about whom this repair is for, where the funds might come from to pay for it, and how environmental aspects, such as stormwater management, are accomplished. But these pointed challenges are a testament to the comprehensiveness of the vision.

Analysis of the 2000 U.S. Census indicated the rise of diverse immigrant suburbs. Eleven million immigrants entered the country in the 1990s alone, and increasingly they migrated directly to gateway suburbs, such that more immigrants – from Latin America, the Caribbean, Africa, Asia, and Europe – live in suburbs than in cities, especially around Chicago, Los Angeles, Miami, New York, San Francisco, and Washington, D.C.[17] Landscape architect Anne Vaterlaus and I have collaborated on design research for retrofits in Hispanic "ethnoburbs," such as our project "Rivera Crossing" for the Mexican–American suburb Pico Rivera, east of Los Angeles. Specifically, we are exploring ways to shift commercial landscapes from consumption

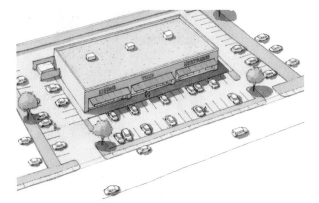

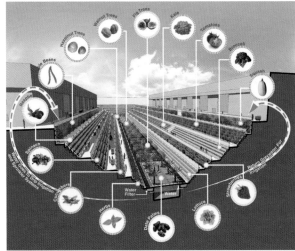

In the 2010 book *Sprawl Repair Manual* town planner Galina Tachieva illustrates dozens of before-and-after examples of her design method, in this case for a retail strip.

In "Rivera Crossing," a 2008–2011 collaboration, June Williamson and Anne Vaterlaus proposed retrofitting a big box power center and warehousing facility in Pico Rivera, California into a suburban landscape oriented around production rather than consumption.

to production by focusing both on growing and process-ing agricultural products while repairing rifts in the local ecologies and on consciously designing these retrofit sites to support a mix of uses, with access to mass transit, for low- and moderate-income suburbanites.[18]

New Urbanists Galina Tachieva and Lee Sobel, now with the Environmental Protection Agency; Georgeen Theodore and Dan D'Oca of Interboro; Paul Lukez; Regional Plan Association urban designer Rob Lane; and design journalist Allison Arieff, a founder of *Dwell* maga-zine, became, with me, the jury for the Build a Better Burb competition.

The design responses of the 2000s to suburbaniza-tion and sprawl embody current responses to a 50-year discourse. The issues of the 1960s and 1970s regarding symbolism in the suburban vernacular and class bias in

design professionals are still with us. Concerns that arose in the 1980s about traditional urban form and density versus car culture and the legacies of urban renewal and the abandonment of city neighborhoods are ongoing. The concern for the decline of public space that was so well articulated in the 1990s also persists, although the terms and conditions of analysis and activism have changed with the emergence of digital, networked culture. And in the 2000s, the discussion has expanded to include the local and the global, viewed simultaneously, necessary because of both rapid urbanization and the local impacts and exchanges due to worldwide migrations of people and flows of goods and capital.

Perhaps, however, we will look back at 2010, the year of the competition, as a watershed in the design discourse about suburbs and suburbia.

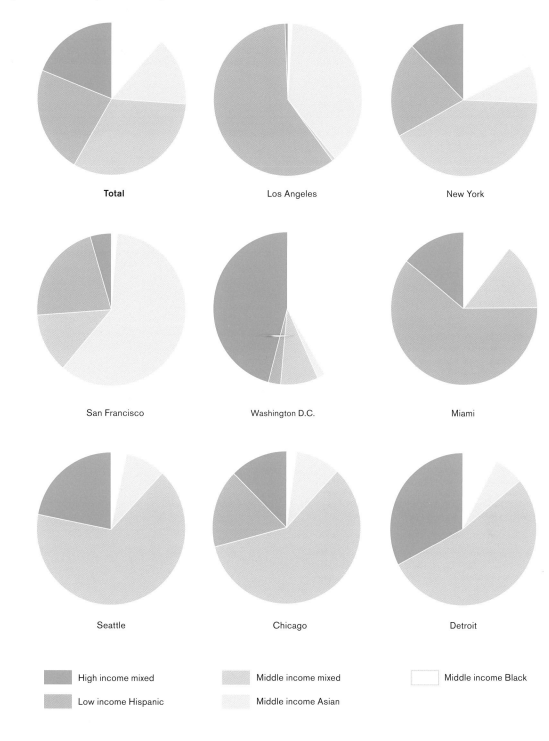

Total

Los Angeles

New York

San Francisco

Washington D.C.

Miami

Seattle

Chicago

Detroit

High income mixed

Low income Hispanic

Middle income mixed

Middle income Asian

Middle income Black

Demographic characteristics of immigrant suburbs for different U.S. metropolitan areas. The growing percentage of suburbs with high numbers of foreign-born residents is socioeconomically and racially diverse.

Source: Based on U.S. Census of Population, 2000. Adapted from Figure 7.2 in Hanlon, B., J. R. Short, and T. J. Vicino, 2010. *Cities and Suburbs*. London: Routledge.

Notes

1. J. B. Jackson published Moore's essay "Toward Making Places," co-authored with fellow University of California at Berkeley faculty Donlyn Lyndon, Sim van der Ryn, and Patrick Quinn, in his fledging journal *Landscape* in 1962. For more on Moore, see Michelangelo Sabatini, "The Poetics of the Ordinary: The American Places of Charles W. Moore," *Places* 19:2(2007):62–71.

2. Robert Venturi, Denise Scott Brown, and Steven Izenour, "From La Tourette to Levittown," in *Learning from Las Vegas*, revised edition (Cambridge, MA: MIT Press, 1977), 152–53.

3. Ibid., 158–59. See also Beatriz Colomina, "Learning from Levittown: A Conversation with Robert Venturi and Denise Scott Brown," in Andrew Blauvelt, ed., *Worlds Away: New Suburban Landscapes* (Minneapolis: Walker Art Center, 2008), 49–69. For a review of "Signs of Life," see Ada Louise Huxtable, "The Pop World of the Strip and the Sprawl," *The New York Times*, March 21, 1976.

4. Robert A. M. Stern, "Garden City Suburbs," *Wharton Real Estate Center Review* 11:2(Fall 2007):84–93. The article was adapted from the keynote address to CNU XV, the annual conference of the Congress for the New Urbanism, Philadelphia, May 19, 2007.

5. Robert A. M. Stern and John Massengale, *The Anglo-American Suburb: AD Profile* (London: Architectural Design, 1981). For a review, see Paul Goldberger, "An Honorable U.S. Tradition of Suburban Planning," *The New York Times*, November 12, 1981.

6. David Mohney and Keller Easterling, eds., *Seaside: Making a Town in America* (New York: Princeton Architectural Press, 1996).

7. For an impassioned summary of this argument, see Ellen Dunham-Jones, "New Urbanism as a Counter-Project to Post-Industrialism," *Places* 13:2(2000):26–31.

8. Doug Kelbaugh, ed., *The Pedestrian Pocket Book* (New York: Princeton Architectural Press, 1989). For a good summary of this history, see Ian Carlton, "Histories of Transit-Oriented Development: Perspectives on the Development of the TOD Concept," IURD Working Paper Series, Institute of Urban and Regional Development, UC Berkeley (Fall 2007).

9. Office for Metropolitan Architecture, Rem Koolhaas, and Bruce Mau, *S, M, L, XL* (New York: Monacelli Press, 1995). See also Jacques Lucan, *OMA–Rem Koolhaas: Architecture 1970–1990* (New York: Princeton Architectural Press, 1991).

10. Koolhaas, *S, M, L, XL*, 977.

11. Douglas Kelbaugh, "Further Thoughts on the Three Urbanisms," in Douglas Kelbaugh and Kit Krankel McCullough, eds., *Writing Urbanism* (New York: Routledge, 2008), 105–14.

12. Michael Sorkin, ed., *Variations on a Theme Park: The New American City and the End of Public Space* (New York: Noonday Press, 1992). Contributors include Trevor Boddy, M. Christine Boyer, Margaret Crawford, Mike Davis, Neil Smith, Edward W. Soja, Michael Sorkin, and Langdon Winner.

13. Margaret Crawford, "The World in a Shopping Mall," in Michael Sorkin, ed., *Variations on a Theme Park* (New York: Noonday Press, 1992), 30.

14. Lee S. Sobel with Ellen Greenberg and Steven Bodzin, *Greyfields into Goldfields: Dead Malls Become Living Neighborhoods* (San Francisco: CNU, 2002). The original study was produced in cooperation with the management consultancy firm PricewaterhouseCoopers.

15. Paul Lukez, *Suburban Transformations* (New York: Princeton Architectural Press, 2007).

16. Galina Tachieva, *Sprawl Repair Manual* (Washington, DC: Island Press, 2010).

17. Bernadette Hanlon, John Rennie Short, and Thomas J. Vicino, "The Rise of Immigrant Suburbs," in *Cities and Suburbs: New Metropolitan Realities in the US* (New York: Routledge, 2010), 132–53. There have been several recent history monographs and dissertations on ethno-burbs, including one on Pico Rivera, by Jerry Gonzalez, "A Place in the Sun": *Mexican Americans, Race, and the Suburbanization of Los Angeles, 1940–1980* (PhD diss., UCLA, 2009).

18. Inspiration for this work is drawn partly from Los Angeles transportation planner and Latino activist James Rojas.

Untitled, 1998–2002, Gregory Crewdson.

Better Suburban Futures

The process of designing better suburban futures might result in the wholesale rejection of the category of suburbia itself, as some have called for, although we are not yet at that point. Suburbia and suburbs remain useful terms, despite the weight of stereotypes. The historic context for change outlined in a previous chapter suggests how suburbia is, and has been, a dynamic condition, as much a cultural state of mind as a set of physical patterns on the land. Readings of suburbia – as culture and as place – are continually shifting, shedding old paradigms and introducing new ones in succession over the past century and a half. We urgently need design professionals and their allies to work in a proactive mode for better, more resilient suburban futures. This chapter introduces promising paths forward.

Lessons Learned from Retrofitting Suburbia Case Studies

In the instructions to entrants for the Long Island Index's Build a Better Burb competition, launched in 2010, designers were asked to consider this question: "How might Long Island's existing downtowns be creatively retrofitted – reinhabited, redeveloped and/or regreened – in ways that are economically productive, environmentally sensitive, socially sustainable, and aesthetically appealing?"

This challenge stemmed from the findings of a decade of urban design research I conducted in collaboration with architect Ellen Dunham-Jones. We began by wondering what was being done across North America with aging and vacant big box stores, dead malls, dying commercial strips, traffic-choked edge cities, outdated office parks, and aging garden apartment complexes. Armed with curiosity and a small grant, we traveled around to find out. In our book *Retrofitting Suburbia: Urban Design Solutions for Redesigning Suburbs*, first published in 2009, we document and analyze dozens of fascinating examples of suburban retrofitting that, taken together, demonstrate the significant potential for profound transformation, over time, of the unsustainable sprawling patterns of late twentieth-century suburbanization.[1]

Three Strategies for Retrofitting

The three main strategies Dunham-Jones and I identified for retrofitting are *reinhabitation*, or various forms of adaptive reuse; *redevelopment*, or urbanization by increasing density, walkability, and use mix; and regreening, from introducing more public space in small parks and plazas to restoring wetland ecologies.

The *reinhabitation* strategy applies various forms of adaptive reuse or reprogramming of older retail sites such as strip malls and big box stores, which can be permanent or temporary. Often reinhabitation results in a shift from private to public use, such as to a branch library or government offices, but it also can engage the entrepreneurial energy of new immigrants and others who open small, community-oriented service businesses.

Retrofitting by *redevelopment*, or the scraping and rebuilding of a campus tissue–type site, such as a shopping mall, office park, or garden apartment complex on a large parcel of land, usually results in transition from a single-use, car-dependent configuration to one that is mixed in use, transit served (or servable), and, often, higher density. Redevelopment can be a way to introduce a new morphology of urban blocks and streets, an "instant urbanism." The transformative proposition is that the new morphology, once established, can permit a process of incremental transformation to unfold over time in a way that the campus tissue could not. It is also conducive to supporting the transition to greater use of modes of mobility that do not depend on carbon fuel, including biking and walking.

The third strategy, *regreening*, can range from the introduction of small civic spaces, parks, and green roofs, to large-scale ecological repair of watersheds and wildlife corridors damaged by decades of suburban development in sprawl patterns. The un-development and de-densification of poorly located commercially developed sites – a land banking of sorts – is an important aspect of retrofitting, to be considered in tandem with the redevelopment and densification of nodes and corridors. Another form of regreening is the suburban farming movement, which promotes the conversion of suburban lawns for vegetable gardens and chicken coops.[2]

These strategies support an ideal of incremental metropolitanism, that is, the gradual emergence, in increments, of a robust and efficient multicentered network of infilled centers and corridors within existing North American metropolitan regions, replacing the pattern of ever-outward sprawl. Often, these approaches are used in combination. All three strategies are important in achieving the primary long-term task of suburban retrofitting: to seek opportunities to adapt and change the underlying urban morphological structure – the pattern on the land of streets, blocks, and lots and the configurations of buildings on them – into more resilient patterns.

How are these strategies implemented? There are regulatory, financing, and other barriers to applying the strategies; these barriers are being systematically addressed by urban actors – local, regional, and national – in creative ways. The following groupings demonstrate a range of already-realized opportunities for retrofitting suburbia toward urban resiliency. These tactics are drawn from lessons learned from my ongoing suburban retrofitting research, lessons that might guide creative design thinking about the next generations of suburban retrofits.[3]

Lot Scale: Boxes, Streetscapes, Housing Choice
The first set of tactics is operative at the scale of a single building or lot, although the total can be more than the sum of the parts in that multiple examples juxtaposed can add up to a larger impact. These tactics include the following:
– Reuse the box.
– Establish a more continuous streetscape with shallow liner buildings.
– Diversify housing choice and price.
– Add new units to existing subdivisions.
– Enhance civic life with small plazas.

The *reuse the box* tactic refers to the adaptive reuse of vacant commercial buildings for new, often community-serving uses, such as libraries or medical clinics, which is socially desirable and reduces waste. In the Denver metro area, two anchor department stores were retained at shopping malls that were otherwise demolished in the early 2000s for public–private mixed-use redevelopment projects. Both stores were built in the 1980s to the same prototype design, a multistory, largely windowless box with chamfered corners. One anchor store, at the large 106-acre town center retrofit Belmar, the former Villa Italia mall, was not demolished and instead was reinhabited as a Leadership in Energy and Environmental Design (LEED)–certified three-story office building, with retail on the ground floor. The other, nearby at CityCenter Englewood, formerly Cinderella City Mall, is now Englewood Civic Center, housing City Hall; light filters in through an art-filled atrium cut through the old building's floor slabs. Other examples of reusing the box include the award-winning Camino Nuevo Charter Academy elementary school in Los Angeles in a former mini-mall, as well as numerous churches, clinics, public libraries, and other nonretail, community-serving uses that have popped up in empty big box stores and strip centers.

The next tactic, *establish a more continuous streetscape with shallow liner buildings*, can be achieved by deploying shallow wrapper buildings around reused box buildings. Shallow one-story liner buildings can complete the street and screen surface parking lots. Mashpee Commons, a retrofit of a strip shopping center on Cape Cod in Massachusetts begun in the mid-1980s, deserves credit for pioneering responses to many of the challenges to conventional suburban development and zoning that are increasingly becoming routine in suburban retrofitting projects. Designers at Mashpee used 20-foot-deep liner shops, leased to local mom-and-pop retailers, around existing parking lots to give a two-sided street presence to the Commons. Liners can also be incorporated into buildings. For example, a structured parking deck might have a street-fronting ground floor liner of small retail shops or artists' studios, 20 feet deep, the depth of one row of parking spaces, such as in Block 7 at Belmar, in Lakewood, Colorado.

The future success of suburbs will hinge on the ability of housing markets to be nimble in response to changing demographics. Demographic trends in the United States include a shrinking percentage of households with children, with an associated increase in the percentage of one- and two-person households, and increases – albeit unevenly distributed – in foreign-born residents and residents from minority groups in suburbs. To respond to these trends, it is essential for suburbs to *diversify housing choice and price*. Varying degrees of housing types, affordability, accessibility, and incentives within rather than between neighborhoods can support greater diversity and access to opportunity in all suburbs. For example, housing for empty nesters and older adults forms a key part of many retrofitting plans in order to allow people to age in place or to be near their families. A key part of this tactic is to introduce and integrate housing choice into existing neighborhoods that are homogeneous in dwelling type.[4]

One example of an innovative housing type that might appeal in many suburbs is The Towers at University Town Center, a 910-bed apartment building in an office park retrofit in Hyattsville, Maryland. The apartment building is located close to transit (bus and D.C. Metrorail) and part-time retail and restaurant jobs. Though not a dorm, the four-bed, four-bath units are optimally designed for sharing by unrelated adults. This building caters to college students and recent graduates, but a similar building type could appeal to single older adults. Researchers in New York City have recently begun to document how the apartment types available in the city (and supported by codes and standards that date back to the post–World War II housing shortage crisis) no longer fit well with current housing demand, as single people looking to affordably share with others or live alone outnumber families seeking the more traditional apartment layouts that the codes are oriented toward. The "Making Room" initiative in New York City in 2011 invited design explorations of a "microloft" housing type, consisting of 300-square-foot or smaller units.[5] The issue of increases in one-person households, and the lack of appropriate legal housing to suit, is just as pressing in suburbs as in center cities.

One more specific tactic to diversify housing choice, and price, is to *add new units to existing subdivisions*. Infilling residential neighborhoods with accessory dwelling units can provide affordable housing choices for singles of all ages and increase residential density without dramatically altering the morphological pattern. A change in zoning can allow the legalization and addition of accessory dwellings, attached or detached in backyard cottages or above a garage, to existing houses and house lots. The benefits, beyond affordability and increasing dwelling unit density, include more housing choice, the opportunity to accommodate immediate or extended family, and greater flexibility in living arrangements.

Several municipalities in the Pacific Northwest have passed widespread zoning revisions permitting detached accessory units. In the early stages of the process, in the late 1990s, in order to gain public support for their initiative, the City of Seattle launched a design competition and built three exemplary demonstration units. After passing a more widespread ordinance, Seattle's Planning Commission and Department of Planning and Development issued a comprehensive "Guide to Building a Backyard Cottage." The winning Build a Better Burb entry "Sited in the Setback," by Meri Tepper, imagines the spatial and social impacts of a gradual buildout of accessory units, conceived as modular building components, in Levittown, New York.

Retrofits also offer opportunities to *enhance civic life with small plazas*. Instead of oversized parking lots or lawns in required setback zones in front of commercial buildings, with landscape to be seen but not occupied, open space can be shaped into small plazas. In downtown Silver Spring, Maryland, a municipal parking lot was transformed into a Civic Plaza, programmed with farmers' markets, music festivals, and an ice skating rink in winter. In an interim stage, the asphalt was temporarily covered with synthetic turf; it became a site not only for picnics and general hanging out but also for a protest gathering in support of free speech in the adjacent lifestyle center, built with public subsidy in the downtown urban renewal district.[6] "Enter\\Shift," by Gordona Marjanovic, is a sensitive design for a greened civic plaza to replace parking lots surrounding the Long Island Rail Road station in the town of Babylon. The innovative, successful Public Plaza Program of New York City's Department of Transportation transforms excess roadway into places to rest and walk, often with just some planters as bollards and surface paint. A better balance can be achieved, using the tools of good design, to find places to support social and civic life of commuters and village center visitors as they transition between trains, bikes, cars, and walking.[7] All should be equally considered modes of transportation. Along these lines, Edgar Papazian's "LIFE Program" proposes a color-coded system of pavement reclamation.

Neighborhood Scale: Block Sizes, Street Types,
Connectivity, and Repair

The second set of tactics redress the neighborhood scale,
operative in the shaping of streets and blocks. These tac-
tics include the following:
– Keep block sizes walkable.
– Use appropriate street types and real, public sidewalks.
– Improve connectivity for drivers, bicyclists, and
  pedestrians.
– Consider future connectivity and adaptability.
– Provide environmental repair by reconstructing wetlands
  and creeks.

For a neighborhood to support mobility modes beyond
private automobiles, it is imperative to *keep block sizes
walkable*. Without careful modulation in retrofitting redevelopment projects, the hybridization of suburban building
types and parking into urban blocks and streets can lead to
oversized blocks and monotonous building fronts. The rule
for a walkable block is a perimeter dimension of no more
than 1,700 linear feet.[8] A typical Portland, Oregon block is
a compact square of 200 by 200 feet, yielding an 800-lin-
ear-foot perimeter, whereas a typical Manhattan block of
200 feet by 600 feet yields 1,600 linear feet. Adding mid-
block pedestrian passages or paseos to supersized blocks
can also increase walkability.

The successful building prototype known as a Texas
donut, so called because of a pioneering series of
examples in that state, consists of embedding unadorned
concrete parking decks in the center of a three- to four-
story "stick-built" residential apartment block (constructed
with light wood framing or light gauge metal framing),
resulting in an inviting streetscape.[9] However, the resul-
tant blocks are somewhat large, just barely walkable in
dimension. Reducing or eliminating parking minimum
requirements and locating residential parking in more
remote locations could increase walkability. There is ample
room for innovation in configuring flexible housing types to
fit into walkable blocks.

The tactic of well-scaled blocks should be wedded to
the tactic to *use appropriate street types and real, public
sidewalks*. Sidewalks are important, though often under-
valued, public spaces. Maintaining their publicness – and
avoiding privatization – while providing comfortably scaled
dimensions for sidewalks should not be overlooked, as it
so often is.[10] I have visited mixed-use suburban retrofits
where the sidewalks seem an afterthought, where the
grading is poorly handled. Sometimes, the sidewalks
appear as discontinuous concrete aprons around buildings; there is awareness that they should be there but not

enough thought about how they might be used. The project
"re-lief" by Kipp C. Edick and Jia-Jun Yeo considers the
issue of small-scale streetscape improvements in suburban
downtowns.

Many suburban streets are overly wide and lack
comfortable sidewalks and crosswalks. In residential
areas within an interconnected street system, an overall
right-of-way of 60 feet with 16-foot sidewalk and tree
planting strips on either side of a 28-foot roadway should
be sufficient.[11] The Institute of Transportation Engineers
2010 manual on designing walkable urban thoroughfares
provides recommended design guidelines for a broad
range of context-sensitive street types. Two dozen states
and many local jurisdictions have passed a version of
"Complete Streets" legislation, requiring transportation
agencies to factor noncar uses of streets and sidewalks
into all projects.[12]

Thinking beyond how walkable blocks and well-scaled
and proportioned street sections add up together, the next
tactic at the neighborhood scale is to *improve connectivity
for drivers, bicyclists, and pedestrians*. For the full gains of
retrofitting to be realized, any redeveloped or reinhabited
node should make connections to the adjacent built fabric,
so that people can walk, bike, or drive shorter distances to
get from any given point A to point B. We must seek ways
to build interconnected street networks to increase walkability, bikeability, and public safety while distributing traffic
loads and reducing overall vehicle miles traveled. "The
21st Century Right-of-Way" proposal by Ian Caine, Derek
Hoeferlin, and their team argues for zoning modifications
to provide easements along commercial strip corridors to
support walkable infill development. The morphology of
suburban strip tissue can be described as elastic, meaning
that there is a loose fit between lot size and configuration
(usually determined by earlier agricultural uses on the land)
and the footprints of chain store buildings built on them.[13]
"The 21st Century Right-of-Way" suggests ways to exploit
this typical condition.

Related to improving connectivity is the tactic to
consider future connectivity and adaptability. If desired
street, bikeway, and pedestrian path connections cannot be achieved when the retrofit is initially designed and
constructed, because of NIMBY (not-in-my-backyard)
concerns or other barriers, easements for future linkages
should be designed in. If desired densities and parking
decks cannot be justified yet, design parking lots as future
building sites. Channel utilities together in the location
of future streets at the outset rather than laying them out
along the shortest paths, wherever they may lie.

The exemplary retrofits of a shopping center into Mashpee Commons on Cape Cod, Massachusetts and of a regional mall into Belmar in Lakewood, Colorado illustrate this tactic. At Mashpee Commons the owners of a neighboring apartment complex were wary of forming a direct street connection, fearful of through traffic, so the master plan includes some gaps between house lots in locations where streets could be connected if and when the neighbors have a change of heart. At Belmar, a strip of land to the east was not part of the retrofitted property, but the new streets align with the grid of the subdivision beyond and could be connected across the strip in the future.

Parking lots in lower-density commercial retrofits can be designed for anticipatory or planned retrofitting, an initiative being explored by environmental lawyer Dan Slone and real estate analyst Lee Sobel of the U.S. Environmental Protection Agency's Office of Policy, Economics and Innovation and a Build a Better Burb juror. Sobel explains, "This is the process of preplanning for tomorrow's retrofit today. There are times when walkable place-based projects may not be possible today. . . . Planned Retrofit embeds many of the techniques of place-making into an auto-oriented development: putting roads in the right place, the infrastructure aligned with the roads, the easements and rights of way, and a few strategic legal considerations. Whatever project gets built today, all of the legal and physical infrastructure is in place for retrofitting in the future when the time is right."[14] In essence, the parking lots can be laid out in a block configuration, with each parking area conceived of as a potential future building site when the development market is receptive to more density and additional uses. The collector lanes between blocks of parking, where below-grade utilities should be placed, can be planted with "street" trees to reinforce the potential.

Suburban retrofits sometimes provide the opportunity to *provide environmental repair by reconstructing wetlands and creeks*, components in the metropolitan watershed that have been systematically erased or diminished by suburban development patterns over time. For example, in the northeastern United States, many malls and strips centers were built on filled swamp wetlands because these parcels were not considered valuable. The ecological functions of these lands were not appreciated. Interstate highways were also often routed over or near suburban wetlands, to avoid disturbing thickly settled areas. Some of these developments on filled land have suffered from poor stormwater drainage in parking lots and occasional flooding, sometimes severe. Retrofitting offers opportunities to repair these conditions, by daylighting creeks and reconstructing areas of wetlands, of benefit not only to the particular property but also to

the entire stormwater catchment area that the wetlands once served, not to mention the animal habitat that can be restored, at least in part.

In the Northgate neighborhood on the north edge of Seattle, a little-used overflow parking lot for a busy regional shopping mall was prone to flooding. The headwaters of Thornton Creek were buried in a large culvert beneath the asphalt, and local environmentalists lobbied hard for daylighting. Developers were also interested in the property, and planners hoped to see more density, because the terminus of a light rail line was planned for the adjacent quadrant of overflow mall parking. The City of Seattle helped broker a win–win solution: a combination of new "soft" stormwater infrastructure in the form of a very sophisticated vegetative bioswale (called, uncreatively, the Thornton Creek Water Quality Channel) and mixed-use development with hundreds of attractive new housing units in Thornton Place, a significant percentage subsidized through an inclusionary housing provision.

The project "Reclaiming Community," by Courtney Embrey and Michael Narciso, similarly promotes ecological repair of excessively paved-over land, in their case of the threatened Hempstead Plains habitat in Nassau County on Long Island, one of the most rapidly vanishing ecological habitats in the world, according to Embrey and Narciso.

Policy: Revising Codes and Standards, Promoting High-Quality Design

This set of tactics is policy based, suggesting ways that retrofitters may engage with the underlying protocols that have directed suburban growth in North America for many decades. Different protocols will produce different results. The tactics in this category are as follows:
– Revise zoning codes and public works standards.
– Invest in durable, high-performance architecture and landscape.

Concerted, coordinated efforts to *revise zoning codes and public works standards* will make it easier to build compact, mixed-use neighborhoods with complete streets and make it harder to build single-use, auto-dependent places. This tactic operates primarily at the level of local government where land use decisions are made. A promising trend is the reexamination of dated zoning codes that require separated uses, deep setbacks, and wide streets. Many of these codes were adopted in suburbs from boilerplate model codes, with little or no calibration for local conditions and practices, and have had the practical effect of guaranteeing an automobile-dependent urban form.

Instead, form-based codes and new, softer infrastructure standards may be adopted.

One laudable example of the successful implementation of a form-based code is along a 3.5-mile stretch of Columbia Pike, in Arlington County, Virginia. The overlay code, adopted in 2003, provides incentives for densification in clearly demarcated districts or nodes along the strip while exerting significant controls on form, such as implementing build-to lines for buildings and setbacks for parking lots. The form-based code consists of a succinct document (seventeen pages for most properties) with three parts that replaces Byzantine legalese with clear diagrams and maps, intended to make the development approval process short and predictable. A regulating plan indicates what type of building can be built in any location and its frontage type to the pike, as well as the aforementioned built-to lines. Building envelope standards govern height, fenestration, siting, and use. Architectural standards recommend materials and configurations of walls, roofs, windows, and doors, although they do not prescribe any particular style. Some architects take issue with these standards, engaging in the usual creative tensions between "civil designers" and "civil editors."[15] Streetscape standards provide recommendations for sidewalks, planting strips, open space, and civic squares.[16]

In the decade since adoption the new code has been highly successful, and efforts are under way to expand its reach, with different standards for the parcels in between the nodal districts already regulated, based on localized conditions and needs, particularly to preserve housing affordability. A proposed streetcar along Columbia Pike is progressing steadily toward implementation. Another pathway toward public works standards reform is local adoption of the practices recommended in the Institute of Transportation Engineers recent manual *Designing Walkable Urban Thoroughfares: A Context Sensitive Approach*, produced jointly with the Congress for the New Urbanism.[17] The project "Bike the Burb!," by Hannah Hesse and Jochen Friedrichs, proposes public works for biking in boxy modular units that can be retrofitted into typical car parking space.

An example of land use policy reform at the state level is the South Carolina Commercial Center Revitalization Act, introduced to the legislature in early 2011. The act would "encourage, but not require, the South Carolina Council of Governments (SCCOG) to adopt model ordinances to enable and encourage the retrofitting of shopping malls and shopping centers into dense, walkable, mixed-use town centers."[18]

Coordinated efforts must also be undertaken to encourage *investment in high-quality design and durable, high-performance architecture and landscape*. The most successful, sustainable and resilient retrofits will be beautiful, durable, culturally significant, and built to meet high standards of environmental performance, both in the open spaces and in the buildings. Solidly built buildings in retrofits should be designed with the capacity to accommodate varied uses, as well as innovative architectural additions and infill over time, complemented with attractive, high-performance landscapes that can function as "soft" stormwater infrastructure.

LEED standards for green buildings and interiors and for neighborhood design set a high bar for energy performance and provide clear metrics — continually reviewed and revised by membership committees — for calculating results. Although one may quibble with the specifics of the point ratings systems and how they might be gamed by plucking the lowest-hanging fruit, it is undeniable that the U.S. Green Building Council and LEED have changed values for the better in the professions that shape the built environment.

The road ahead may require designers to become even more knowledgeable than they already are about real estate financing and pro forma financial statements so as to find the most effective ways to argue for the market value and potential returns — both economic and ecological — of good design and durable, high-quality materials and methods.

New Ideas Suggested by Build a Better Burb

The Build a Better Burb competition for the suburban region of Long Island was launched by the nonprofit Long Island Index in the spring of 2010, with the goal of attracting and stimulating new design thinking as applied to suburban challenges, some specific to the Long Island Region but most common to much of North American suburbia. Analysis of the seven winning proposals and the fourteen notable submissions included in this book suggests several innovative new ideas and strategies, investigated at various scales by the design teams.

Several of the winning projects proposed interventions at the regional scale, recognizing that the futures of the nearly three million residents of Long Island were inextricably linked, not only within the two-county region, with its limited open space and freshwater resources, but also within the larger New York metropolitan area of twenty-two million inhabitants, the Northeast megaregion of fifty-two million, and, indeed, the North American continent and the globe. As ecological researchers have increasingly recognized, about 75 percent of the land area of the globe must now be defined as anthropogenic biomes or anthromes, that is, defined and shaped by human systems. Less than 25 percent of the globe's land mass remains as "wild land" biomes, mostly in the earth's coldest and driest regions. The anthrome paradigm, recently defined by environmental scientist Erle Ellis and his research colleagues, suggests that humans have the primary responsibility for planetary stewardship, as permanent managers of the limited and renewable resources of our planet.[19]

Regional Scale: Carbon, Water, Governance Structures
Three new regional-scale design and planning tactics suggested by the competition are as follows:
– Use soft infrastructure for large-scale carbon
   sequestration.
– Privilege the conservation of freshwater aquifers in
   shaping long-term growth.
– Radically reconceive fractured suburban governance
   structures to reduce energy use and significantly
   improve efficiency.

The first innovative tactic, *use soft infrastructure for large-scale carbon sequestration*, is offered in "Building C-Burbia," a winning proposal by landscape architect and City College of New York professor Denise Hoffman Brandt, with Alexa Helsell and Bronwyn Gropp. In the proposal, the designers provide a soft infrastructure system for short-term biomass storage and formation of long-term soil carbon reservoirs in the suburban landscape, the "mixed settlement" anthrome identified by Erle Ellis. The C-Burbia system – C stands for carbon – was "designed to disperse across the urban field, latching onto existing physical structures, policy, and funding mechanisms to optimize carbon cycle performance and amplify the experiential intensity of suburban landscape." How is this "latching onto" achieved? By opportunistically co-opting all sorts of existing and potential suburban landscapes – highway verges, arterial medians, street trees and lawns, plantings on vacant lots and building roofs – to become active, measurable carbon sinks.[20] Policies could be adapted so funding that would normally go to plantings as "beautification" could instead be directed toward plantings selected to maximize carbon sink potential, with little or no new expenditure.

The second regional-scale tactic, *privilege the conservation of freshwater aquifers in shaping long-term growth*, is explored in "Long Division," proposed in the winning

collaboration between the Network Architecture Lab at Columbia University and PARC Office. As the title suggests, the team divided Long Island into two primary zones, based on infrastructural and ecological factors. Much, though not all, of the less-developed northeastern end of the region, which lacks full sewage infrastructure even though it sits on one of the most productive aquifers in the United States, is identified as a "no-growth zone" where conservation of the aquifer is to be privileged. All new growth would be directed toward emergent dense centers to the southwest, closer to the center city, in places reasonably well served with transit, water, and waste infrastructure. This tactic echoes the idea of urban growth boundaries but instead is focused around preserving a vital natural resource – freshwater – and has the result of suggesting an archipelago of denser development rather than a bounded, continuous territory.

Maintaining fresh drinking water supplies in metropolitan regions is a tall challenge. Depleted and polluted aquifers can be replenished, sometimes with treated sewage, but it is far wiser to preserve existing water resources and to shape land uses accordingly. Environmentalists have documented the devastating effects on water resources of harmful detergents leaching out through subdivision septic tanks and cesspools in the 1950s and 1960s.[21] Suburban commercial development in filled wetlands has compromised the performance of many regional watersheds, exacerbating damaging flooding. The iconic postwar planned community of Lakewood, California (see "Context for Change"), for example, is participating along with many other southern California communities in extensive efforts to pump in treated water to replenish the aquifer, compromised with salinated or brackish water because of depletion over many decades. The obvious route to avoiding this type of costly technological fix is to strenuously avoid compromising the freshwater resources in the first place. Many other sprawling, heavily suburbanized regions are confronting the limits to growth posed by threats of freshwater scarcity, including Las Vegas, Phoenix, and Atlanta. The collision course between freshwater resources and continued global urbanization will become an increasingly pressing concern worldwide in coming years.

The third regional-scale tactic, *radically reconceive fractured suburban governance structures to reduce energy use and significantly improve efficiency*, is proposed in "LIRR: Long Island Radically Rezoned," the winner of an online "people's choice" voting process in the Build a Better Burb competition. The scheme was submitted by architect Tobias Holler, architecture professor at the New York Institute of Technology, in collaboration with

Ana Serra, Sven Peters, and Katelyn Mulry. The designers propose applying closed-loop principles to systems of water, energy, waste, and food on a macro scale; to ease implementation, they propose replacing the current, inefficient governance structure of the region (Long Island consists of over 430 individual government entities whose jurisdictions overlap in complicated ways). They suggest replacing this crazy quilt with a new structure organized around proximity to mass transit stations. In other words, they propose to rigorously and radically retrofit the region into a network of more densely settled, transit-oriented village nodes, which they call "Smart Cells." The connective land area in between these cells would be conserved for wildlife habitat, human recreation, agriculture, and renewable energy production. Their scheme illustrates the possibility of achieving 50/50 balance between densely settled land and open areas.

Although the premise for radical redrawing of municipal borders in "LIRR" may seem far-fetched, legal scholar Myron Orfield has argued forcefully for new regional governance structures that transcend local jurisdictions, for both equity and efficiency.[22] In the wake of the Great Recession of the late 2000s, local governments in the United States were seriously crippled and the inefficiencies of small size became apparent. Sharing and consolidation are on the recovery agenda in many suburban regions. What is new here is the role design might play in conceptualizing, organizing, and representing these alternative, potentially more equitable, efficient, and resilient governance structures.

Downtown Scale: Use Mix, Leveraging Culture, Schools as Infrastructure, Suburban Agriculture
Four new tactics suggested by the winning Build a Better Burb schemes that operate at the scale of a suburban "downtown" or center include the following:
– Robust rethinking of the use mix to challenge and rethink the live–work–play triad.
– Using transit infrastructure to network cultural institutions together.
– Harnessing the potential of the locational network of public schools and school buses.
– Implementing suburban agriculture at scale.

The first tactic, *robust rethinking of the use mix to challenge and rethink the live–work–play triad*, is offered in a number of the competition schemes, a clear recognition of the importance of increasing the diversity of building types and sizes in order to support suburban resilience. Although the live–work–play triad has been useful in conceiving of projects that combine three predominant and potentially

profitable suburban development types – market-rate apartments or townhouses, ground-floor retail shops, and Class-A office space – it leaves out many other use possibilities and reinforces a narrow reading of suburban lifestyles and needs as synonymous with white-collar, upper-income workers and their families.

In "LIRR: Long Island Radically Rezoned," Holler and his colleagues suggest new uses for revitalized downtowns. They suggest that each downtown will comprise centers in a new network of bounded governance jurisdictions where most residents would live. They use a vast mix-and-match menu of tactical strategies, creatively informed by the case studies in *Retrofitting Suburbia* and other sources, to illustrate the potential of these denser centers. They provide the fanciful, memorable names of "fix-a-block," "re-center," "mall chopper," and "resi-dense" for these urban form-making tactics.

Similarly, for "Long Division," the Network Architecture Lab and PARC Office propose a set of four growth zones – densified downtowns – in the transit-rich southwest of Long Island. All new development would be directed to these zones while lands over the aquifer would be conserved and, over time, "voided." They propose a rich set of new types for these centers, designed in response to needs for housing, open space, and productivity; the new types are hybrids, sensitive to the considerations of segments of the area's population who are not well served by the predominant "real estate product types" of detached houses, retail strips, and office parks, namely seniors, aspiring minorities, recent immigrants, and artists and artisans. The new combinations they suggest are playful but also provocative. "Urban elders" combines housing, a community center, and a botanical garden; "micro-industry dealership" combines machine assembly and distribution, company housing, and office space on retrofitted car dealerships; and "urban backyards" add barbecue pits to a small public park, suggesting compensation for the loss of private backyards. Although well-designed, durably constructed urban buildings can and should be dimensioned and designed to accommodate a variety of uses over a long life span, rather than the cheap suburban commercial types for single uses that have been designed to last no longer than the term of their initial financing, usually less than 20 years, it is immensely useful to the conversation to visualize and imagine what some of the new use combinations might be.

As progressive real estate developer and scholar Christopher Leinberger argues, suburban form in the last generation has been built largely to conform to a limited menu of nineteen standardized real estate types, conceived as distinct "asset classes." Investment analysts have tracked these classes for the past few decades and have developed confidence that they can reasonably predict rates of return for these investments, sight unseen. Real estate investment trusts, publicly traded on Wall Street, tend to specialize in only one or a few of these types, which are predominantly single use and include build-to-suit office, neighborhood retail center, big-box anchored retail, mobile home park, business and luxury hotel, and entry-level housing.[23] In order to get access to Wall Street financing for the types of mixed-use projects that support walkable urbanism, Leinberger argues, it is vital to provide some level of standardization — that is, to create new asset classes — for the types of mixed-use developments many would like to see built in walkable suburban downtowns and nodes.[24]

In addition, new standards are needed within government-subsidized and insured programs, in the United States Department of Housing and Urban Development, the Federal Housing Administration, Fannie Mae, and Freddie Mac, to help level the financing playing field for mixed-use development. Not attempting these reforms, he argues, is tantamount to ensuring that mixed-use suburban projects, limited to the private equity market, remain expensive and rare. The Congress for the New Urbanism is aggressively pursuing an initiative to implement discussions on these topics with federal government partners, specifically the conception of a new set of asset classes, to be labeled "live/work/walk." If these efforts are successful, we may soon see new opportunities for architects, planners, and developers to form common cause in making more complex development types more common and more affordable to finance.

A second new tactic is *using transit infrastructure to network cultural institutions together.* As planner and business scholar Richard Florida asserts in several popular books, the ability of places to attract creative knowledge workers, a group he dubbed "the creative class," can play an instrumental role in economic development when successfully courted.[25] Several of the noteworthy submissions selected for this volume were innovative in this area, including "Bethpage MoMA P.S. 2," by Nelson Peng, Zhongwei Li, and Yang Wang, and "Rail Park," by Bergmann Associates.

In "Bethpage MoMA P.S. 2," the designers envision a network of vibrant new arts institutions in transit-served downtowns, intended to build cultural capital. Recognizing that suburban industrial parks with high vacancy rates reproduce the conditions that spawned the revitalization of city arts districts such as SoHo, West Chelsea, and Long

Island City in New York, Fort Point Channel in Boston, and Bergamont Station in Santa Monica — namely, cheap, high-ceilinged space — they propose transit- and art-oriented development. The Museum of Modern Art's second home, called P.S. 1, is lodged in a repurposed public school building in the New York City borough of Queens. Peng, Li, and Wang suggest that although their proposed site in the Nassau County town of Bethpage, with a large but struggling industrial park, is conveniently linked to the central city by rail, the artists working there "could feed into building a community that is less about the commute to NYC and is about truly living in the local."

"Rail Park" is based on the adaptive reuse of surplus components of the transit infrastructure itself by the arts community and as repositories of cultural history. The designers recognize that rail yards and tracks, though used to connect places to one another, can also function as unsightly hard boundaries and socioeconomic dividers in the places they pass through. The saying that someone comes from the wrong side of the tracks is evidence of this phenomenon. Urban highways have had a similar effect. Along with encouraging connectivity across these types of boundaries with additional infrastructure such as at-grade crossings, underpasses, bridges, and decking, the reuse of space dedicated to servicing transit infrastructure that is surplus may provide a significant opportunity to increase a sense of place and history in older, leapfrogged suburban communities.

A third tactic at the nodal or downtown scale is *harnessing the potential of the locational network of public schools and school buses.* A challenge for fixed commuter transit systems in low-density suburbs is what is called the last mile problem, that is, the challenge for transit commuters to get to their homes from the transit station. My own family confronted this problem when moving in the early 1980s to a suburb of Boston from London, where we had become accustomed to relying on frequent and convenient bus and rail service. My parents limited their search to houses within walking distance of commuter rail stations, a highly novel priority in the United States at the time and a source of amusement and frustration to the real estate agents they dealt with. Who aspired to be a one-car family when they could afford two? Unfortunately, we soon caved to the necessity of the built environment we were living in and bought a second car.

Until recently, the last mile problem has been handled in North American suburban transit planning by constructing large no- or low-fee park-and-ride facilities around stations, encouraging commuters to deposit vehicles all day long. These fixed, parked cars occupy space that would otherwise be ideal for transit-oriented development. The perceived need to provide convenient parking at stations led in the past to the demolition of otherwise viable downtown buildings in many older suburban areas. More recently, transit planners in suburban areas have tended, counter to recent thinking on urban resiliency, to locate commuter park-and-ride stations in locations convenient to highways and remote from existing development, places where ample parking could be built cheaply.

The brilliant, potentially transformative key insight of the winning scheme "SUBHUB Transit System" by DUB Studios is to propose a feeder transit system for the last mile problem. Recognizing that elementary public school sites tend to be evenly distributed in the suburban residential fabric and embedded within it, serving subsets of the local population, they propose these sites as hubs of the subsystem. Furthermore, school buses could be co-opted as transit shuttles for commuters and goods in the hours when they are not transporting kids. Many suburban areas that eschew publicly subsidized mass transit actually already have it and could use it better. Of course, it would be healthier if more kids walked to school, but the dendritic road configurations of residential subdivisions, especially of recent vintage, are a significant impediment, even when the will is there.

The "HuB-URB" (not to be confused with "SUBHUB") scheme by Jing Su addresses the problem of suburb-to-suburb or intra–Long Island transit. Most commuter rail systems around the world are spoke and hub. "HuB-URB" proposes cross-island connections, restoring links that decades ago were provided by trolley and interurban lines, most long since dismantled in favor of car-based infrastructure.

The fourth tactic in the section is *implementing suburban agriculture at scale*. Regreening strategies are already being used in many suburban neighborhoods, exemplified by the trend explored by conceptual artist and guerrilla gardener Fritz Haeg in his "edible estates" project, in which, people voluntarily eschew the fertilizer-intensive suburban ideal of the perpetually (and unnaturally) green lawn in favor of cultivating their yards for edible produce.[26] Historically, the covenants, conditions, and restrictions of residential subdivisions that aspired to maintain middle-class status often explicitly forbade vegetable gardening, at least in the front yard, because cultivation for "self-provisioning" suggested economic need and hence a class status of precariousness that might reduce property values. Dryer lines for laundry were similarly controlled, as indicative of the scrabbling hand-to-mouth existence one was meant to leave behind in the old urban ethnic enclave.

The question here is whether and how suburban agriculture might be scaled up or implemented at a scale or size sufficient to be economically competitive in providing locally grown products that could be brought to market in the "subhub" feeder networks discussed earlier. Local neighborhood community associations might do the job, along the lines proposed in "Upcycling 2.0" by Ryan Lovett, Patrick Cobb, and John Simons, all still graduate students when they entered the competition. They propose that members in the association might pool and manage small funds for local community improvements and amenities, including an agricultural network.

"AgIsland," by a team from Parsons Brinckerhoff, led by Tom Jost, explores this theme, envisioning "replacing office parks with organic farms, fed by AgTrain, a conveyor connected to processing, distribution and rail to connect . . . to dense centers where goods are sold." They propose that AgTrain can convey waste to soil-mixing and waste-to-energy plants, to provide organic soils to farms and alternative energy to the community. Meanwhile, the office park functions are relocated to commuter rail–served downtowns where, perhaps, they should have been built in the first place.

Lot Scale: Aging and Intergenerationality, Cottage Industries, Income Pooling

Three final intriguing tactics suggested by the winning Build a Better Burb schemes, tactics that operate at the scale of individual suburban lots and the buildings on them, include the following:
– Completely new housing configurations and types for aging-in-place baby boomers and intergenerational households.
– Reintroducing cottage industries and associated housing types.
– Introducing bottom-up mechanisms to support infill community improvements.

The tactic of providing *completely new housing configurations and types for aging-in-place baby boomers and intergenerational households* is driven by the imperative of changing demographics. Many analysts assert that the current North American housing market is oversupplied with large detached homes, designed for families with children. The market is undersupplied with options for single people, families without children ("empty nesters" and couples who don't yet have children or never plan to), and nonfamily households (unrelated adults sharing a dwelling, or roommates).[27] This state of affairs is a tremendous opportunity for architects to work with developers and planners to conceive of flexible new ways for people of all ages and incomes to live together. These new ways could differ from the standard product types that have conventionally made up the housing market, which many, unwisely, are waiting to see cranked up to full steam again in the former boomburbs, subsequently the epicenter of the foreclosure crisis.

Whereas Meri Tepper's "Sited in the Setback" proposal, discussed earlier, illustrates the potential of prefabricated detached accessory dwelling units to intensify an older postwar subdivision such as Levittown, the proposal "Re:Define the Good Life," by interior architect Sara Hill, suggests the retrofit of a dead shopping mall into residential apartments. Just as the abandoned industrial buildings of city neighborhoods such as SoHo and Tribeca in New York were transformed for loft living, the suburban retail sheds discarded by chain retailers, when not recyclable for local retailers or community-serving uses, could be used for housing. Whereas the midcentury discourse about the good life inspired modernist architects to rethink family life through designs for free-flowing open-plan houses with large ribbons of windows that brought the outside in, architects today can respond robustly to the implications of increased longevity, population growth through immigration, and the many types of household configuration, including intergenerational, that can result.

The proposals "The Articulated Strip," by Judith De Jong and David Ruffing, and "REpark," by Scalar Architecture, suggest designs to add new modular housing to the parking lots of thriving malls. "The Articulated Strip" proposes architecture that is deliberately open-ended, deploying a primary structural system in concrete that would allow additional floors and remodeling over time. "REpark" specifically suggests that housing for older adults be installed on shopping mall parking lots. The buildings could be built in modular sections, in an incremental fashion, expanding in footprint in response to demand. Assistance — medical, social services, recreation — could then be conveniently provided at the mall.

Another tactic with great potential is *reintroducing cottage industries and associated housing types*. "The Living Market," designed by prolific planning academic Emily Talen and Sungduck Lee of Arizona State University, takes up the cause of revitalizing suburban downtowns by proposing new infill housing of the age-old "shop–house" type, variants of which are found in many cultures across time.[28] They propose that this new housing, built over existing retail space or in new units fronting a central marketplace, be reserved for market vendors engaged in cottage industries, their families, and their employees. This proposal endorses the proposition by Patrick Condon, in his "seven

rules for sustainable communities," that most light industry is not noxious, dirty, or particularly noisy and doesn't need to be zoned separately from housing; as he puts it, "most new jobs don't smell bad."[29] This proposition, which flies in the face of a century of zoning convention in developed economies, is eminently practical and could introduce tremendous economic flexibility. "HIP Retrofit," by Anderson/ Kim et al., proposes a similar approach to localizing economic activities and scaling down workplaces, for an industrial park setting rather than a downtown. Instead of the indirect subsidy of the homebuilding industry through the mortgage deduction in the U.S. tax code, deductions for home-based industry and production should be expanded and encouraged, along with relaxation of use-based zoning restrictions.

Finally there is the idea developed in "Upcycling 2.0," by Lovett, Cobb, and Simons, for *introducing bottom-up mechanisms to support infill community improvements*. Many of the Build a Better Burb entries touched on this idea, suggesting the use of social networks, digital devices, neighboring, and home-based businesses to suggest ways that suburbanites could collaborate at the local level. "Upcycling 2.0" proposes the clever tagline "making your ecological footprint within walking distance" to suggest the local, bottom-up nature of their approach to building social and economic capital in suburban neighborhoods with the small-scale financing mechanism of income pooling. This can be done while preserving the qualities of suburban life that people tend to value: privacy, access to a backyard, and home ownership. New community improvements built through the income pooling mechanism — a basketball court, a pet hydration station, communal composting bins — would be fully compatible with these values. This idea is also compatible with the groundswell of innovation in the recessionary moment from young designers and planners engaged in "tactical urbanism," "do-it-yourself urbanism," and other spontaneous interventions.[30]

All these ideas and tactics can and should be explored, elaborated, and tested. Additional ideas can be developed, new partnerships forged, and new narratives shaped. The time for working together to design a more resilient suburban future is *now*.

Notes

1. Ellen Dunham-Jones and June Williamson, *Retrofitting Suburbia: Urban Design Solutions for Redesigning Suburbs* (Hoboken, NJ: Wiley, 2009, updated edition 2011).

2. Suburban domestic farming and animal husbandry can often meet significant regulatory hurdles, in homeowners' association covenants, conditions, and restrictions and restrictive R-1 zoning regulations.

3. Some of these ideas were first outlined and illustrated in June Williamson, "11 Urban Design Tactics for Suburban Retrofitting," written in 2011 for the Build a Better Burb website: http://buildabetterburb.org /article.php?aid=145.

4. See Henry Cisneros, Margaret Dyer-Chamberlain, and Jane Hickie, eds., *Independent for Life: Homes and Neighborhoods for an Aging America* (Austin: University of Texas Press, 2012).

5. Making Room was sponsored by the Citizens Housing and Planning Council and the Architectural League of New York. See http://making roomnyc.com. Subsequently, the New York City Department of Housing Preservation and Development invited developers to submit proposals for a prototype project of microloft units to be built on a parking lot owned by the New York City Housing Authority in Kips Bay, Manhattan. The project will receive regulatory waivers. See http://www.nyc.gov/html/om /html/2012b/pr257-12.html.

6. June Williamson, "Protest on the Astroturf, July 4, 2007," in Christopher Niedt, ed., *Social Justice in Diverse Suburbs: History, Politics and Prospects* (Philadelphia: Temple University Press, 2013).

7. For details on the New York City Department of Transportation Public Plaza Program, see http://www.nyc.gov/html/dot/html/sidewalks /publicplaza.shtml.

8. Michael Mehaffy, Sergio Porta, et al., "Urban Nuclei and the Geometry of Streets: The 'Emergent Neighborhoods' Model," *Urban Design International* 15(2010):22–46.

9. See projects in and around Dallas developed by Post Properties and designed by RTKL, such as Addison Circle and Legacy Town Center in Plano.

10. A point made by Anastasia Loukaitou-Sideris and Renia Ehrenfeucht in *Sidewalks: Conflict and Negotiation over Public Space* (Cambridge, MA: MIT Press, 2009).

11. Patrick M. Condon, *Seven Rules for Sustainable Communities: Design Strategies for the Post-Carbon World* (Washington, DC: Island Press, 2010), 54–59.

12. For more on the National Complete Streets Coalition, which advocates the adoption of policies to ensure "that transportation planners and engineers consistently design and operate the entire roadway with all users in mind — including bicyclists, public transportation vehicles and riders, and pedestrians of all ages and abilities," see http://www .completestreets.org/.

13. For a classification of conventional suburban morphological tissues, see Brenda Case Scheer, "The Anatomy of Sprawl," *Places* 14:2(Fall 2001):28–37.

14. E-mailed comments to author from Lee S. Sobel, February 29, 2012.

15. Mark C. Childs, *Urban Composition: Developing Community through Design* (New York: Princeton Architectural Press, 2012), 20–21.

16. For more on the revitalization of Columbia Pike, including links to the form-based code, see http://www.columbiapikeva.us/.

17. Institute of Transportation Engineers and the Congress for the New Urbanism, *Designing Walkable Urban Thoroughfares: A Context Sensitive Approach: An ITE Recommended Practice* (2010). Available at http://www.ite.org/css/.

18. South Carolina Commercial Center Revitalization Act, State Bill H. 3604.

19. Erle C. Ellis, Kees Klein Goldewijk, Stefan Siebert, Deborah Lightman, and Navin Ramankutty, "Anthropogenic Transformation of the Biomes, 1700 to 2000," *Global Ecology and Biogeography* 19:5(September 2010):589–606. See http://ecotope.org/anthromes /paradigm/.

20. A carbon sink is a natural environment, such as a forest or ocean, with the ability to absorb and store more carbon dioxide from the atmosphere than it releases.

21. Adam Rome, *The Bulldozer in the Countryside: Suburban Sprawl and the Rise of American Environmentalism* (New York: Cambridge University Press, 2001). See also William Cronon, "Silent Spring and the Birth of Modern Environmentalism," foreword to Thomas R. Dunlap, ed., *DDT, Silent Spring, and the Rise of Environmentalism: Classic Texts* (Seattle: University of Washington Press, 2008), ix–xii.

22. Myron Orfield, *American Metropolitics: The New Suburban Reality* (Washington, DC: Brookings Institute, 2002).

23. Christopher B. Leinberger, *The Option of Urbanism: Investing in a New American Dream* (Washington, DC: Island Press, 2007), 49–57.

24. The Sprawl Retrofit Initiative of the Congress for the New Urbanism has identified challenging the limited standardization of new, mixed-use real estate types or "products" as a priority. Related are the Congress for the New Urbanism initiatives to work with Fannie Mae and Freddie Mac to create a new, mixed-use asset class and efforts to work with HUD to expand mixed-use components in the housing projects they fund. See http://www.cnu.org/sprawlretrofit.

25. See Richard Florida, *The Rise of the Creative Class: And How It's Transforming Work, Leisure, Community and Everyday Life* (New York: Basic Books, 2002), and, more recently, *The Great Reset: How the Post-Crash Economy Will Change the Way We Live and Work* (New York: Harper, 2010).

26. Fritz Haeg, Will Allen, and Diana Balmori, *Edible Estates: Attack on the Front Lawn*, 2nd revised edition (New York: Metropolis Books, 2010).

27. Arthur C. Nelson, *Reshaping Metropolitan America: Development Trends and Opportunities to 2030* (Washington, DC: Island Press, 2013).

28. See Howard Davis, *Living over the Store: Architecture and Local Urban Life* (New York: Routledge, 2012).

29. Patrick M. Condon, *Seven Rules for Sustainable Communities: Design Strategies for the Post-Carbon World* (Washington, DC: Island Press, 2010), 87–88.

30. "Spontaneous Interventions: Design Actions for the Common Good" was the theme of the U.S. Pavilion commissioned by Cathy Lang Ho of the Institute for Urban Design at the 2012 Venice Architecture Biennale, with dozens of participants interested in interventions in suburbs and cities including Rebar, initiator of PARK(ing) Day; Jason Roberts and Andrew Howard of Team Better Block; James Rojas with his Place It! community-planning workshops; and Mike Lydon of Street Plans Collaborative, author of the self-published *Tactical Urbanism Handbook*. See http://www.spontaneousinterventions.org.

Exemplar: Building a Better Burb on Long Island

Build a Better Burb 2010: _____ Instructions_____ and Commentary_____

Following is the full text of the original instructions, or design brief, provided to designers wanting to enter the Build a Better Burb competition for Long Island, sponsored in 2010 by the Long Island Index, a project of the Rauch Foundation. Drafting an effective brief is an essential component of sponsoring a successful design competition.

The eight members of the competition jury, Allison Arieff, Daniel D'Oca, Robert Lane, Paul Lukez, Lee Sobel, Galina Tachieva, Georgeen Theodore, and June Williamson, met in Garden City, New York in late June 2010 to review the more than two hundred submissions to the competition. Excerpted in the margins are some of their general comments, provided that summer and more recently, in 2012, in response to a follow-up questionnaire.

For additional documentation of the competition, visit buildabetterburb.org.

Three of 156 downtowns and railroad stations on Long Island, with thousands of acres of greyfield land.

The time for cautious thinking is over. New visions are needed for the next generation of suburban centers.

Suburbia is not as built out as it seems. Consider the mapping of *8,300 acres* of opportunity – vacant parcels and parking lots – in the many small downtowns of the country's "first suburbs" on Long Island. On the occasion of the release of these revealing new interactive maps, the Long Island Index invites all architects, urban designers, planners, students, visionaries and everyone else interested in shaping our suburbs' future to help us "Build a Better Burb." This ideas competition seeks bold design proposals for retrofitting underutilized asphalt in suburban downtowns into innovative and surprising new uses, forms and urbanisms.

Roughly equivalent to the area of Manhattan south of 50th St., 8,300 acres is a lot of land. It is still, however, only 1.1% of the land mass of Nassau and Suffolk Counties. By building in a new way on *this* land, rather than elsewhere on Long Island in the old way, there is tremendous opportunity to address the contemporary challenges of suburbia, by shifting focus to the prewar landscape of small towns and mass transit that languished during decades spent constructing highways, shopping malls, dream-home subdivisions and far-flung office parks. How might Long Island's existing downtowns be creatively retrofitted – redeveloped, reinhabited and/or regreened – in ways that are eco-

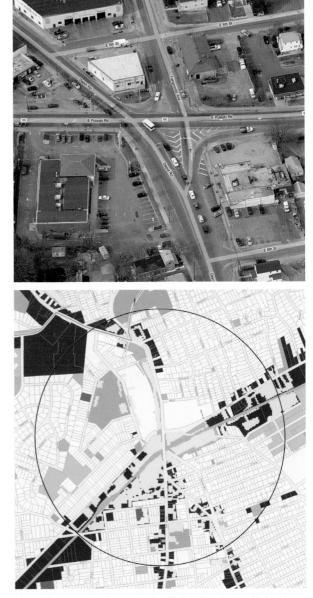

Map of downtown Levittown, Nassau County, New York, showing land use within a half-mile radius of the center. Bright yellow indicates acres of opportunity along Hempstead Turnpike.

Map of downtown Huntington Station, Suffolk County, New York, showing land use within a half-mile radius of the center. Bright yellow indicates acres of opportunity around the railroad station.

nomically productive, environmentally sensitive, socially sustainable, and aesthetically appealing?

Building suburbia in the old way is no longer working. Statistical indicators show that Long Island is facing several pressing challenges: to build affordable housing and greater housing choice, especially for rentals; to reduce car dependency and congestion; to bring Long Island's diverse communities together in a shared public realm; to improve equity and access to opportunity for all; to meet the needs of retiring baby boomers who wish to age in place; and to fight the "brain drain" of younger residents who don't see a future here and leave.

There has been a crisis of imagination, and your bold new ideas are urgently needed. There should be no preconceptions about what is or is not possible. What would you do on these acres of opportunity? Build a car-free community for thousands? Plant an oasis of urban agriculture? Produce renewable energy and provide well-paying green jobs? Use landscape systems to repair ruptures in regional ecologies? Introduce armatures to enhance public space and the civic realm?

The best ideas, designs, images and videos will be selected as finalists by a diverse jury of distinguished academics and professionals and exhibited on the website. An important goal of "Build a Better Burb" is to widen the debate about Long Island's future; therefore, finalists' projects will be publicized in a broad media campaign over the summer of 2010 to encourage the public to vote and comment for a "People's Choice Award." Other exciting initiatives to disseminate the work of the finalists are in the planning stages. Cash prizes totaling $22,500 will be awarded.

_____The Challenge_____

With assistance from the Regional Plan Association and the CUNY Mapping Service at the Center for Urban Research, the Long Island Index recently added a new layer focused on the downtowns to our interactive online map of Long Island – the only publicly available, comprehensive source of mapped data for the two counties, home to almost 3 million residents. A couple of examples of the 156 downtowns and train stations that were identified, surveyed and mapped give a sense of the opportunities for good design to make a real difference:

This competition celebrates the extraordinary energy that is at present being directed towards solving the long-neglected problems of suburbia as planning and design phenomena. "Sub-urban Design" is emerging as field worthy of continued investment of interdisciplinary and creative energy.
Paul Lukez

I think this competition framed the issues well: segregation, the lack of housing and mobility options, and political balkanization pose a serious threat to Long Island.
Daniel D'Oca

The greatest contribution of the competition is to draw attention to the inevitable transition from auto-oriented environments to human-scale, walkable and diverse places, and the re-scaling of car-oriented urbanism to mixed-use, finer-grain fabric.
Galina Tachieva

"Suburb" has outlived its usefulness as a descriptive term – and as a model for future planning, at least in its current incarnation. Suburbs continue to be designed for homogeneity even though they're no longer homogeneous at all.
Allison Arieff

I was most excited by projects that engaged the lived conditions of the suburbs, rather than rejecting them. Instead of considering the suburbs as a "tabula rasa," several of the winning projects worked with, and built upon, the everyday landscapes that most Long Islanders call home.
Georgeen Theodore

It was good to see that many ideas were daring yet rooted in common sense. Sometimes the boldest idea is to be realistic and to challenge the existing status quo of policy, regulation and development inertia that promotes sprawl. Nevertheless, the entries were ambitious and broad-gestured, such as proposing transit connectivity for the whole island, greenway corridors sequestering carbon, new agricultural belts, and strategies for saving the local aquifer. Many of the projects were innovative and polemical in nature, stirring the imagination and painting a new picture of the densified, redeveloped suburb: younger, cooler, more diverse, more interesting, and with greater economic, cultural and social potential than the usual suburban stereotype.
Galina Tachieva

The range of solutions does point to a systems-thinking approach: one can't consider housing without considering jobs, and transit, and smart growth, and so forth, and how they influence one another within a whole.
Allison Arieff

What would you propose for the 69 available acres along Hempstead Turnpike in iconic Levittown, where only 3% of the housing units are multi-family, 21% of the population is over 55 and virtually no new housing has been built in decades?

Or what about the 74 acres in downtown Huntington Station, where the Long Island Rail Road station serves an average of over 10,000 riders per day?

Successful solutions may range widely in scale, although you are asked to site your proposal in one or more of the 156 mapped downtown areas. You can propose something *small*, such as an energy-producing bus shelter or a repurposed parking spot. You could propose something *medium*, such as an innovative infill building or a small urban farm on a vacant lot. A big box store could be adaptively reused as intergenerational housing while the parking lot is co-opted as a civic park, or a bicycle station. You could think *big*, and design a mixed-use plan for an entire block, strip shopping center, or historic downtown. Or you could think *extra-big*, and design at the scale of regional infrastructure: to introduce new mobility systems, to manage water, habitat and sewage, to generate renewable energy, or to engage in environmental repair.

Proposals may be prototypical, or customized to a particular downtown. Use your imagination, skills, insight and creativity to help Long Island, and other similar aging suburbs throughout the North American continent, to boldly envision a future that is exponentially better! (A reminder: this is an open call for bold new ideas, not an awards program for actual Long Island projects in process, of which there are many commendable examples.)

_____ Background _____

A Very Brief History of Long Island
In the late 19th and early 20th centuries, Long Islanders lived in hamlets, villages and suburban towns throughout the island, linked to New York City primarily by the Long Island Rail Road. Many worked in agriculture and fishing; others operated local businesses or commuted to the city by rail. There were also numerous large private estates, belonging to wealthy New York industrialists. The downtown commercial districts were small but vibrant community hubs, with shops, cinemas, a variety of businesses, and stations for train and streetcar lines. By the 1930s

Most of the winning submissions tackled this challenge at the scale of larger systems – environmental, economic, transportation, overall settlement patterns – which is appropriate and exciting.
Robert Lane

While the submissions were full of creative solutions, I wish more directly addressed equity issues.
Daniel D'Oca

There are many new strategies generated by this competition that could and should be tested in suburbs around the country, thereby addressing important issues that impact the sustainability of our country's quality of life and the environment.
Paul Lukez

Five general themes distilled from the winning projects:
1. Infrastructure Repositioned
Implication: Work with LIRR to consider mixed traffic on their lines. This happens in some parts of the region already and is not uncommon in other parts of the region. Issues will be overall capacity, safety.
2. Larger Natural Systems Explored
Implication: Promote planning and regulatory initiatives, such as best-practice passive storm water management, that reinforce the underlying natural systems, especially watersheds.
3. Larger Economic Systems Explored
Implication: State, county and local governments should experiment with incubating new kinds of industry. Interest in urban farming and local production suggests that agriculture is a sector where this kind of experimentation should be considered. Several of the schemes are useful for imagining what this might look like.
4. Real Mixed Use
Implication: Reduce conventional limitations on use. Consider more sophisticated tools such as performance-based zoning, subject to the administrative capacity of the municipality.
5. Incremental Change
Implication: Remove conventional limitations on density subject to community tolerance and administrative capabilities.
Robert Lane

The contestants searched for solutions based on policy and regulations, but also physical design. They explored the possible relationships between the isolated, single-use elements of sprawl, and tried to connect them, weave them together, and retrofit them to create an urbanism at a human scale, where walkability is central. It was good to see that there was a whole range of proposals (some of which did not make the finalists' list) that were very explicit about the quality of the public realm, the shape and dimensions of civic spaces, and how existing and retrofitted buildings relate to each other.
We remain optimistic that a number of these ideas will prove the skeptics wrong and become reality, making Long Island a better place for its

Nassau and Suffolk Counties had a combined population of less than 500,000 residents.

But the island's boosters imagined a far different future. In preparation, Robert Moses had begun the construction of thousands of miles of parkways and bridges, later followed by interstate highways. In the postwar era of mass suburbanization, lubricated by federal loan insurance programs, farms and large estates were bulldozed and subdivided for residential development, creating a new, dominant landscape of tract homes while providing entrée to the American Dream for hundreds of thousands families leaving urban immigrant enclaves in Brooklyn, Queens and the Bronx. In Levittown, the most well known of these communities, more than 17,000 houses were constructed between 1947 and 1951. The locus of commerce and entertainment shifted from the old downtowns to new shopping malls and strip centers.

The population of the two counties swelled to 2 million by 1960 and is now approaching 3 million, with most of the growth in the past 50 years occurring in Suffolk County. More farms, private estates, and large airfields were converted to residential subdivisions and office parks. Industrial plants, once a source of good jobs for thousands, like Grumman in Bethpage, builder of the legendary Apollo Lunar Module, are now largely a thing of the past.

Problems and Potentials of "First Suburbs"
Like suburbs across North America, especially the so-called "first suburbs" that were built out in the post World War II period, Long Island is facing several pressing inter-related needs. The best submissions will find creative potential in addressing these problems through better use of the land assets of the historic downtowns and train station areas:

Providing Housing Choice and Affordability
There is a severe shortage of affordable housing on Long Island. In 2000, home values were *three times* household incomes; today, even with the burst of the real estate bubble, they are *five times* household incomes. What about renting? On Long Island, only 17% of the housing stock is for rent. And what of the baby boomers, who may wish to downsize from larger homes, without leaving their communities?

Stemming the "Brain Drain"
Lack of housing choice is contributing to an exodus of young people, aged 25–34. Where are they going? Anywhere but here, it seems. Without a young, educated workforce, businesses are leaving too. What might bring back the younger workers – Richard Florida's "creative

current residents while attracting new investment and the younger generations.
Galina Tachieva

In early 2012, almost 2 years after the competition, the jurors were contacted and asked to
reflect on a series of questions about the competition for the Long Island region and the more
general challenge of designing more resilient
suburban futures. Here are their responses:

Build a Better Burb was a timely competition
that asked all the right questions, most important
among them, How do we increase housing and
transit options for Long Islanders? I think some
really great ideas came out of the competition,
ranging from the feasible to the fantastical. It
was really inspiring to see so much creative
thinking applied to an issue that I don't think
architects talk about enough.
Daniel D'Oca

One of my most vivid memories was that the
competition created genuine interest and
excitement, not only within the local community
of Long Island, but also nationwide and even
abroad among students, academics, design
professionals, and the media. This enthusiasm
was proof of the importance of the competition's
topic – how to solve the predicament of our
sprawling suburbs.
Galina Tachieva

The competition demonstrated that an architectural competition can go beyond being an
interesting design exercise for architects and
designers. By being tied to important issues
(social, economic and civic), public awareness
of the associated problems and solutions can be
raised. This competition was very successful in
that way, calling attention to the issues thanks
to a well-organized outreach process. But this
effort would not have been as successful if not
for the timeliness of the topic, especially in light
of the impact that the economic recession has
had on suburbanites and their communities.
Paul Lukez

Many proposals sensibly advocated for mixing
uses at higher densities. This approach is
certainly valuable; however, in the future, I'd like
to see more architects, urban designers, and
planners creatively addressing the everyday,
auto-oriented spaces between single-use, low
density residential "patches" rather than relying
on tried and tested formulas for developing
mixed-use town centers. These in-between
zones of strip shopping centers, big boxes, and
office parks are the de facto public landscapes
of suburbia and are ripe for rethinking.
Georgeen Theodore

The competition offered a wide range of proposals, some based in transforming building types,
while others suggested regional or ecological
strategies. As a kind of catalog of strategies,

class" – or help them stay? Revitalized downtowns, with
places to live, work, socialize, and walk, are sure to help.

Car-Free Mobility

Long Island already has an extensive commuter rail system,
the Long Island Rail Road. Largely built out by 1900, it has a
"spoke and hub" organization, with a main terminus at Penn
Station in New York City, and does not service north–south
trips across the island. Over time, downtown buildings
adjacent to stations were demolished to increase parking for
commuters. Can these downtowns be reborn to encourage
Long Islanders to leave their cars at home or better yet, not
need to buy a car, because everywhere they need to go is
within easy access on foot, bike or by public transit? Can the
surviving pre-automobile historic built fabric in these downtowns – mixed in use and walkable – be better leveraged to
achieve this goal?

Equity, Access and Public Space

One of the most intractable problems on Long Island is the
degree to which it remains segregated by race and ethnicity
along boundaries drawn in the 1940s and 1950s. The US
Census has found that Long Island is the third most segregated suburban region in the country. It is a region of strikingly
separate and unequal communities. Can good design help to
bridge these divides? We believe it can; shared public and
civic space in downtowns can bring people together across
lines of age, race, ethnicity and class.

The problems facing Long Island are severe and timid
ideas won't help to turn the tide. By no means are we suggesting the bulldozing of what exists. Instead, we encourage
tapping the underutilized land capacity in the downtowns
and revitalizing the historic built fabric that is already there.
Long Island is and will remain suburban, with much land
fixed in stable residential neighborhoods of detached homes.
However, suburban form needs added flexibility to adapt to
future needs. So, with this competition, we wish to focus on
what we can add, remodel, and repurpose to realize the latent
potential of Long Island's many downtowns. Change is the
only way forward.

The time for cautious thinking is over.
We invite you to begin your process
of envisioning and designing the next
generation of retrofits for Long Island
downtowns!

__Opportunities in Long Island Downtowns_____

Where to begin? If you are familiar with Long Island, delve into
the Long Island Index's Interactive Map (www.longislandindex

The competition jury, gathered to review submissions, in late June 2010.

they are by themselves useful and indicative of the current thinking found in the profession about what should and could be done in the suburbs.
Paul Lukez

The need to infill and otherwise re-stitch the suburban landscape where possible, will mean thinking about the limits of urban agglomeration in the suburbs: to what extent can the suburbs start to perform like cities in terms of intensity of land uses, mixing of land uses, mobility and communication? This may mean re-thinking suburban mixed use: mixed use in the suburbs may have to move beyond the idea of an office park with several adjacent businesses, and even beyond the idea of vertical or stacked mixed uses (residential over retail or office). As in the denser parts of the city, mixed use may need to become a temporal as well as physical condition with the same spaces or buildings capable of being re-used for different activities at different times of the day – the kind of *flexible use* strategies we see in cities.
Robert Lane

For a large segment of the population the prototypical suburb is no longer economically or ecologically sustainable. Economics might force people to abandon their suburban communities, leaving them entirely behind. In other places, the consolidation and compression of suburban footprints might yield a new kind of metropolitan texture, allowing for the emergence of more open space between newly constituted suburban nodes.
Paul Lukez

A large challenge to the retrofit process is that of time. The time involved to educate communities, developers, and local governments about the concept of suburban infill redevelopment. The time to assess and prioritize parcels and districts for retrofit consideration. The time to rezone or

maps.org) to locate the acres of opportunity in the downtowns of Nassau and Suffolk Counties. In addition to mapping vacant land in the downtowns, the maps include layers on land use, population, housing, and education, as well as orthophotos.

To see the "greyfields" layer on the map, click on the "Downtown" tab at the left column. Use the pull down menu at the map's upper left to zoom to specific downtowns.

Jury

Allison Arieff is Editor of *The Urbanist*, the magazine of SPUR (San Francisco Planning & Urban Research), and is a regular contributor to the *New York Times*, *The Atlantic Cities*, and *Wired*. Arieff is author of the books *Prefab* and *Trailer Travel: A Visual History of Mobile America*.

Daniel D'Oca is Design Critic in Urban Planning and Design at the Harvard School of Design, Assistant Professor of Art History, Theory & Criticism at the Maryland Institute College of Art, and Principal and co-founder of Interboro Partners, an innovative New York–based architecture, planning, and research firm.

Robert N. Lane is Senior Fellow for Urban Design at Regional Plan Association and a founding Principal of Plan & Process LLP. Lane's work focuses on the relationship between transit, land use and urban design in urban and suburban settings. Research activities at RPA include Redesigning the Edgeless City, an initiative funded by the Lincoln Institute for Land Policy.

Paul Lukez, FAIA, is principal of Boston-based Paul Lukez Architecture and author of *Suburban Transformations*.

Preparations to review the 200+ submissions.

re-code land, buildings, and roads. And the time it takes for such redevelopment to occur.
Lee S. Sobel

I think multiple scales and timeframes are needed [for change], because there are multiple problems. There are people – senior citizens who want to age in place, for example – who need change now. . . . But bigger changes like creating walkable, mixed-use environments, de-Balkanizing government, and many of the other things proposed by entrants to Build a Better Burb obviously require a lot of time.
Daniel D'Oca

Sprawl repair will be an incremental and opportunistic improvement of our suburban landscapes and will happen first in places where economic potential, political will, and community vision converge. There will be small, tactical, grassroots interventions that will show what can be done cheaply and fast; there will be bigger, more ambitious projects initiated by the private sector, taking advantage of changing markets and demographics, building upon the need for walkable environments, mixed use and amenities in suburban sprawl. Thirdly, there will be public-sector initiatives, at multiple scales.
Galina Tachieva

Planners should be sensitive to the criticism that they (or we, since I am a planner) are elitist.
Daniel D'Oca

To truly build better burbs, the messaging must be clearer, the projects must involve the communities involved, and the designs might do well to follow the maxim of industrial designer Raymond Loewy known as MAYA (most advanced, yet acceptable). We will win no supporters by presenting visions of suburbia that completely erase the conventions that so many Americans hold so dear. The current anti-urban rhetoric equates

The book proposes strategies for transforming suburbs into more sustainable and habitable environments, with a unique identity strongly linked to the landscape. Lukez has taught at MIT, Washington University, and Roger Williams University.

Lee S. Sobel is the Real Estate Development and Finance Analyst at the US EPA's Office of Sustainable Communities. Sobel's work focuses on issues related to real estate development that achieves smart growth goals and outcomes. He is author of *Greyfields into Goldfields: Dead Malls Become Living Neighborhoods*.

Galina Tachieva, AICP, is Partner at Duany Plater-Zyberk & Company, Architects and Town Planners (DPZ). Miami-based Tachieva is author of the *Sprawl Repair Manual*, a book outlining scalar methods for the retrofit of auto-centric suburban places into complete, vibrant communities.

Georgeen Theodore is an architect, urban designer, and Associate Professor at New Jersey Institute of Technology's College of Architecture and Design, where she is the Director of the Infrastructure Planning program. She is Principal and co-founder of Interboro Partners, an award-winning New York City–based architecture and planning research office.

June Williamson, competition advisor and jury coordinator, is Associate Professor at the Spitzer School of Architecture of the City College of New York. She is co-author of *Retrofitting Suburbia: Urban Design Solutions for Redesigning Suburbs*.

Bus poster, designed by Ten Times.

Computer workstations for public voting for the People's Choice Award were set up in public libraries.

density with the end of freedom. Approaches put forth must be innovative but must also assuage concerns that someone is trying to stamp out the American Dream.
Allison Arieff

Every suburban region should have a Build a Better Burb competition. It's a great model that should be exported.
Daniel D'Oca

Credits

Sponsor

The Long Island Index is a project that gathers and publishes data on the Long Island region. The Index does not advocate specific policies. Instead, our goal is to be a catalyst for action, by engaging the community in thinking about our region and its future.

Specifically, the Index seeks to:
— Measure where we are and show trends over time
— Encourage regional thinking
— Compare our situation with other similar regions
— Increase awareness of issues and an understanding of their interrelatedness
— Inspire Long Islanders to work together in new ways to achieve shared goals

The Long Island Index is funded by the Rauch Foundation, a Long Island–based family foundation that supports innovative and effective programs in the non-profit sector.
— Ann Golob, Director
— Nancy Rauch Douzinas, Publisher

Interactive Maps
Steven Romalewski, director of the CUNY Mapping Service at the Center for Urban Research

"Place to Grow" Report
Regional Plan Association

Public Relations
Deanna Morton and Robert Simkins, InfiniTech

Winning and Noteworthy
Competition Schemes

Rather than seeking a solution to a localized problem in only one town on Long Island, many of the Build a Better Burb winners and finalists designed systemic proposals, applicable at the larger regional scale or replicable in numerous settings. Although each project's particular scales of operation are chosen to suit the themes and issues at hand, each manages to tackle the shared suburban challenges of environmental, economic, transportation, and overall settlement patterns that a broad scope allows. Even when details of a solution for a single location are offered, they are always intertwined with a sense of place making and system changing that goes beyond the local, into the regional, the national, and even the global realms.

Although each project stands on its own, when they are placed side by side we gain a fuller realization not only of the problems that Long Island and North American suburbs in general face but also of how ambitious the varied solutions necessary to fix them could be. Whether radical in physical scale or subtly revolutionary in concept, we need a packed kit of ideas, a full deck of cards, to design for a more resilient suburban future – large beside small, systems layered on systems, and natural mixed with human-made. Given the suburbs' expected and almost institutionalized homogenizing effect on the landscape – public, private, built, and natural – deployment of a matrix of uses and ideas is the only way to shake up the 'burbs.

Illustrated on the following pages, in full, are the seven winning schemes from the competition. The fourteen noteworthy schemes selected here each highlight a specific tactic of suburban transformation. Taken together as a set they offer a series of inventive, imaginative, and often laudably practical solutions to problems that many suburbs across the world share to one degree or another.

Project Strategy Matrix

Strategy	Sited in the Setback	Upcycling 2.0	AgIsland	Building C-Burbia	SUBHUB Transit System	Long Division	LIRR: Long Island Radically Rezoned	The Living Market	Reclaiming Community	re-lief	The 21st Century Right-of-Way	The Articulated Strip	Re:Define the Good Life	REpark	Rail Park	Bethpage MoMA P.S. 2	HIP Retrofit	Enter\\Shift	HuB-URB	LIFE Program	Bike the Burb!
Social Networks and Bottom-Up Tactics		**X**								x					x					x	
Modular Building	**X**												x	x							x
Alternative Energy Production			x				**X**														
Ecological Repair				**X**		**X**	x			**X**											
Transforming Zoning						x	**X**				**X**										
Adaptive Reuse of Building													x		x		x				
New Uses for Schools					**X**																
Streetscape Elements										**X**											
Supporting Diversity		x				x		x	x												
Financing Tools	x	x																		x	
Multiunit Housing	x	x				x		x					x								
Innovative Building Types	x	x			**X**							x		x							
Walkability and Bikeability			x							x	x				x				x	x	**X**
Transit-Oriented Development (TOD)			x						x					x	x	x			x		
Cultural Capital and the Arts														**X**	**X**						
Infill Development	**X**					x					x	x					x	x			
Supporting Local Economies					x			**X**									x				
Housing Choice for Seniors	x													**X**							
Landscape Improvements				**X**											x			x			
Suburban Agriculture		x	**X**	x			x	x	x												
New Mass Transit Networks		x			**X**									x					**X**		
Strengthening the Public/Civic Realm		**X**				x												**X**	x		
Retrofitting Office and Industrial Parks		**X**															**X**				
Retrofitting Shopping Centers		x					x				**X**	**X**	x								
Retrofitting Auto Infrastructure				x						x	x									**X**	x

> Winning schemes   > Noteworthy schemes

Sited in the Setback: Increasing Density in Levittown
Meri Tepper

Summary

Sited in the Setback cogently explores the vast potential of rezoning for accessory dwelling units ("granny flats") to increase housing choice within existing residential neighborhoods.

Themes

Infill development, modular building, multi-unit housing, housing choice for seniors, innovative building types, financing tools

Description

This project reconsiders planning and construction possibilities for the first ring post-suburban neighborhood of Levittown, New York. When treated as flexible, and not sacred ground, first-ring suburban lots can be rezoned to include accessory dwelling structures. Allowing additional dwellings on existing lots gives homeowners options to accommodate extended family or to earn additional income through renting. Redefining traditional notions of setback, orientation to the property line, density and infrastructure creates a community that offers more options, to this generation and the next.

Untapped Economic Potential

A renovated Levittown house on a quarter acre of land sells for around $400,000. (An original 1947 Levitt house of 750 sq. ft. sold for $7,000.) The convenience of the commute into New York City and good school systems keep the demand for this area high. Because of the one-dwelling per lot rule ("R-1" zoning), homeowners have no way to benefit monetarily from their property unless they are willing to sell their houses and move away from the community.

High Property Values Prevent Buying-In

The average young person who grew up in Levittown cannot afford to buy a house in the neighborhood. As a result, children are unlikely to return even though the community offers young families many benefits and conveniences.

Aging Population

The population of postwar suburban neighborhoods like Levittown is generally older. With increased home operational costs associated with aging, these homeowners in particular are looking for ways to obtain revenue from their high-value property without having to move. Many are also looking for opportunities to have their children or grandchildren close at hand to contribute caregiving.

Energized Density

In this dense post-suburban setting, landscaped rear and side setbacks are maintained as the conventional boundary between residences. Landscape will still be the accepted boundary between the single-family houses, but with "Sited in the Setback" the language shifts from that of

yard and fence, to that of garden room and utility zone. The ecological footprint per capita in the neighborhood is reduced, while doubling the residential dwelling density of the first ring suburbs, by incorporating diverse sustainable technologies in a new approach to infrastructure.

Modular Diversity

Instead of relying on the traditional agents of sub-urban development – timber, labor, machinery, time and cost – this proposal collapses these variables by exploiting the advantages of the modular building industry. House construction is considered as an assembly of rooms, that expands and contracts according to individual needs. Specifically designed modular units can be configured in numerous ways to accommodate different scales of expansion and new construction.

Jury comments

Compactly designed accessory buildings built in the back yards of the original Levittown prototypical home, creates not only affordable housing options, but creates a new neighborhood fabric, denser and more varied. The dream lives on!
– Paul Lukez

This submission was refreshingly clear. It presents a very sensible way to open suburbs like Levittown to non-family households.
– Daniel D'Oca

The proposal is unique with its ideas for multigenerational living and attracting younger residents by providing affordable yet sophisticated housing options, with flexibility for growth of the proposed units and even integration with other generations.
– Galina Tachieva

By using Levittown as a template for repurposing and sub-urban infill development techniques, this community is once again offered as a model for other first-generation suburban communities that want to continue growing in a sustainable fashion. Who says there are no second acts in America?
– Lee S. Sobel

Biography

Meri Tepper, AIA, LEED BD+C, received undergraduate and graduate degrees in architecture from the University of Virginia, where the ideas for this project originated as her masters thesis. Ms. Tepper is a project architect at Ryall Porter Sheridan Architects in Manhattan and currently serves as director of communications for the Women in Architecture Committee of AIA New York.

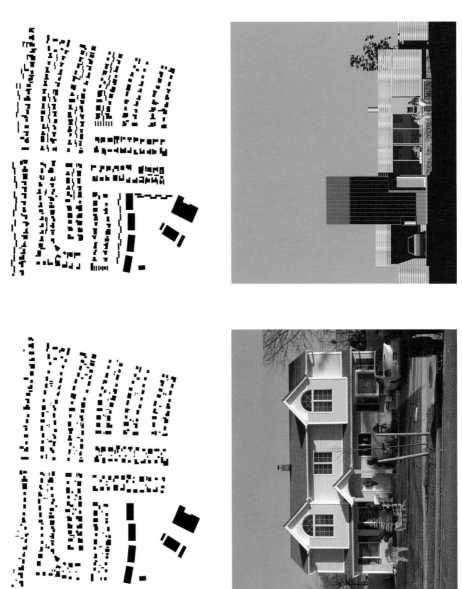

Proposal

2011

1947

1/2 mile radius of downtown Levittown

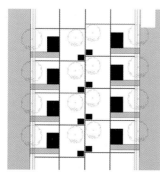
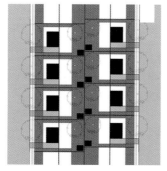
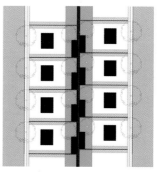

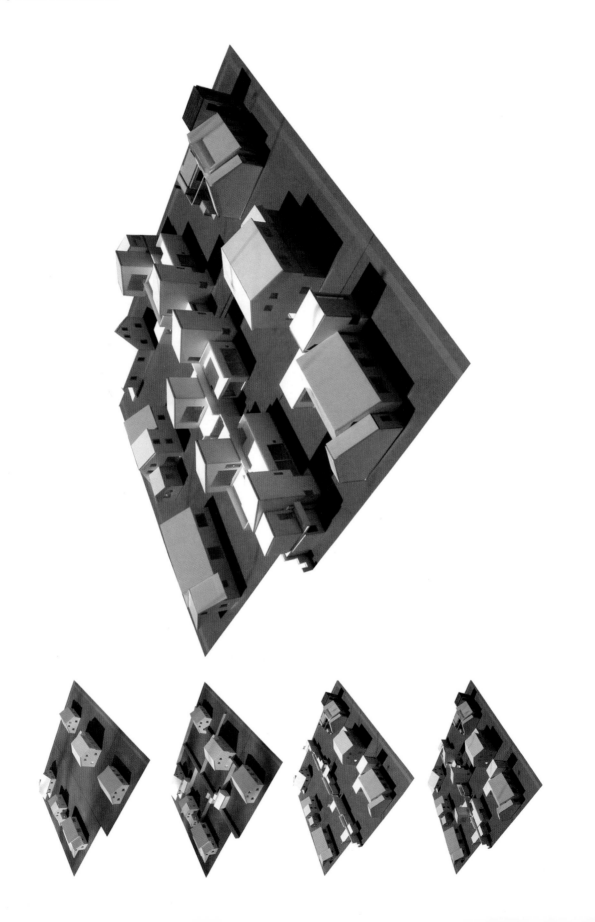

Ground Level   Second Level   Roof

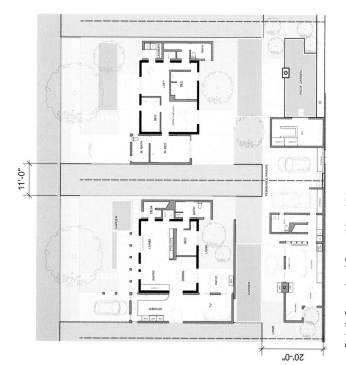

Detail–Ground and Second Level Plans

20'-0"

11'-0"

Upcycling 2.0
Ryan H. B. Lovett, Patrick Cobb, and John B. Simons

Summary

Upcycling 2.0 introduces an intriguing "bottom-up" financing mechanism of income pooling to support infill community improvements, amenities and multiunit housing options.

Themes

Strengthening the public/civic realm, bottom-up tactics, innovative building types, multiunit housing, financing tools, supporting social diversity, suburban agriculture

Description

Upcycling 2.0 is an incremental development approach that combines the positive innovations from both urban centers AND suburban neighborhoods. We refute the idea that density and privacy are mutually exclusive.

Through the strategic market driven acquisition and re-appropriation of property, our proposal encourages interaction and desirability via new community associations that pool and manage funds for community improvements and amenities. This in turn closes economic, environmental, and social loops, while increasing civic participation, awareness, and accountability. There would be a direct correlation between your money and your neighborhood.

Our proposal targets the ubiquitous suburban typologies: the single-family detached house, strip mall, train station, street medians, big boxes, and vast seas of parking lots. By employing a series of different re-appropriations of these typologies, three distinct zones emerge over time: an agricultural network that follows major auto-oriented developments, a mass transit-oriented network would create regional scale economic centers, and finally a series of mixed-use neighborhood enclaves, which feature new public amenities that minimize the need for extra car trips.

The new strategy can be deployed on two fronts: The private sector can slowly acquire privately owned property, and in turn set up new rental types and housing associations, and the public sector could incentivize new development and mandate all new construction be more mixed-use and promote land-use equity.

This bottom-up parcelized approach organically creates a myriad of densities, architectural styles, scales, affordability levels, and ultimately a unique identity that can change over time.

Jury comments

The project title is misleading; this is less upcycling than an HOA with a conscience.
– Allison Arieff

Upcycling 2.0 is bold, addresses financing, and employs a creative, optimistic reading of the suburb and its building blocks, which it proposes to combine in interesting ways.
– Daniel D'Oca

This project builds on existing suburban typologies to create exciting new hybrids – such as the big box + high school – that would densify Long Island's landscape and invent new forms of public space.
– Georgeen Theodore

What is unique about this project is how the team tied the development of new building typologies to financing and development models, incrementally transforming the suburbs over time.
– Paul Lukez

Realistic and practical ideas such as an income stream diagram, collective mailboxes, and community cooking stations are combined with more radical ideas in the form of undulating greenbelts covering existing parking lots with stacked, mixed-use buildings above them. An impressive theme throughout this multilayered entry is the attitude toward infrastructure – whether a parking lot or a highway, they are treated as elements of a shared civic environment that need to be rethought and reused.
– Galina Tachieva

Biographies

Ryan H. B. Lovett is a committed researcher and designer of the built environment with a mission to bring the architecture, planning, and development communities closer together. He recently graduated with master's degrees in architecture and real estate development from Columbia University, where he received an Honor Award for Excellence in Design. He currently works at SHoP Architects in New York.

Patrick Cobb has been a project designer with Laguardalow Architects for 6 years. With advanced training in real estate development and architecture at Columbia University, Mr. Cobb is engaged with designing and planning mixed-use commercial projects around the world.

John B. Simons is a recent graduate of the MArch program at Columbia University. He is now working on complex, large-scale projects at Kohn Pedersen Fox Associates in New York.

The Process

01 Formation of Community Improvement Association

Initiatives determined by democratic vote

Board of Elected Representatives hold meetings
Each major stakeholder at least one board member

C.I.A members and board Work together to Determine how to best Reposition / Redevelop Properties

Non-Profit / Tax-Exempt Status
C.I.A

Local Residents
Priority Low-Interest loans
Vote, raise their earnings for new amenities

Local Bank
Priority Low-Interest Loans
Gain Potential Small Business & C.I.A Investments

Local Government
Provide Streamlined Planning Procedure
Enable Tax Incentives or Tax Exemption
Input elected official serves as C.I.A board member

Local Developers
One time Development Fee
Potential Manage / Operation of Properties
Health / Leases, Rent Collection
Contract Maintenance role

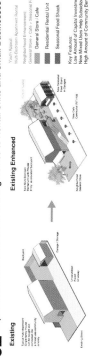

02 Aquisition and Conversion of Existing Homes to Rental Units and Small Businesses

Existing

Existing Enhanced

Youth Appeal
Multi Bedroom Apartment Rental
Neighborhood Enhancement
General Store + Cafe + Seasonal Food Site

General Store / Cafe
Residential Rental Unit
Seasonal Food Shack

Key Features:
Low Amount of Capital Investment
New Mixed Uses Help Subsidize Rents
High Amount of Community Benefit

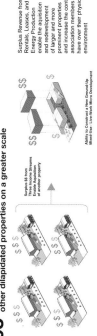

03 Pool membership dues, rental incomes, and lease incomes to aquire and convert other dilapidated properties on a greater scale

Surplus $$ from Three Income Streams Enable Acquisition of another property

Surplus Revenue from Rentals, Leases, and Energy Production enable the acquisition and redevelopment of larger and more prominent properties and increase the control association members have over their physical environment

Ability to Construct a New Ground-Up Mixed-Use / Live-Work Micro Development

04 Repeat Steps 2-3 to increase access to locally produced food, semi-public space, and other community association services like free wi-fi or waste management.

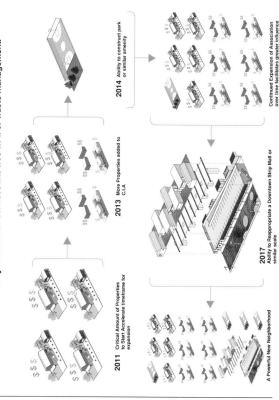

2011 Critical Amount of Properties to Start Accelerate timeframe for expansion

2013 More Properties added to C.I.A

2014 Ability to construct park or similar amenity

Continued Expansion of Association over time facilitates greater influence

2017 Ability to Reappropriate a Downtown Strip Mall or similar scale

A Powerful New Neighborhood

The Concept

A Long Island Needs to become "Glocalized"

Global

Glocal

Local

Individual
Specific
Climate
Historical Fabric
Family / Friends

Collective
General
Infrastructure
Manufacturing
Technology

"The union of global and local denominating the territory of interactions, connflicts, and relations between the individual and the collectivized"

Localized Infrastructure
Localized Manufacturing
Less need for Travel
More Individualistic
More Specific city in Place
Amplification of Historical Fabric

B Vertically Integrated Networked Neighborhoods

Agriculture
Single-and Multi- Residential
Multi-and Residential
Retail Commercial
Manufacturing Freight

C Bottom Up Development Approach

2017   2020
2012
Now

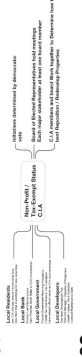

D Pooled Income Stream for Public Benefit

Rental Income

Rental Income

Membership Dues

E New Development Concentrated Along LIRR, With Zones Catering to Specific Industry

Making your ecological footprint within walking distance.

Semi-Autonomous Cottage Industry Network
Eco Tourism Centered Economy
Fishing / Preservation Economy
Agriculture Centered Economy

Development Networks
Long Island Rail Road
Major Automobile Roads
Transit Oriented Development Network (.5 walkability indicator)
Conservation / Antigrowth Zone

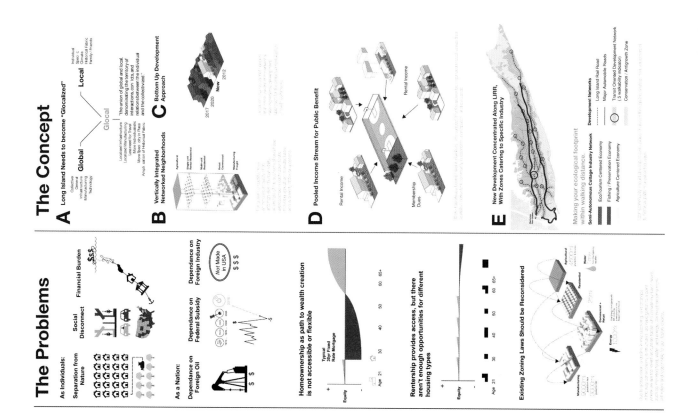

The Problems

As Individuals:

Separation from Nature

Social Disconnect

Financial Burden
$$$

As a Nation:

Dependance on Foreign Oil

Dependance on Federal Subsidy

Dependance on Foreign Industry
Not Made in USA
$ $ $

Homeownership as path to wealth creation is not accessible or flexible

Typical 30yr Fixed Rate Mortgage

Equity   + / −
Age 21   30   40   50   60   65+

Rentership provides access, but there aren't enough opportunities for different housing types

Equity   +
Age 21   30   40   50   60   65+

Existing Zoning Laws Should be Reconsidered

Agricultural
Water
Residential
Commercial
Energy
Manufacturing

Potential Amenities

Suburban Furniture

Excercise Station / Stoop

AREA LIGHT

Collective Mailboxes

Community Composting

Portable Seating + Playing Surfaces

BUS SHELTER

STREET VENDOR

Pet Hydration Station

BOTTLE FILLING STATION

Community Water Tower / Lounge

Community Cooking Station

POTABLE WATER

Impromptu Performance Space

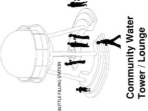

The Mechanism

The relationship between new income streams can be closed to provide and perpetuate the expansion cycle of development while also being environmentally sensitive

Community Amenities / Park

Park

Pool

$ Profits

Rental Unit
Rental Unit
Rental Unit

Community Free WiFi

$ Profits

Office Area
Office Area

Agricultural Area

$ Profits

General Store
Food Shack

Fresh Produce

'Grey' Water

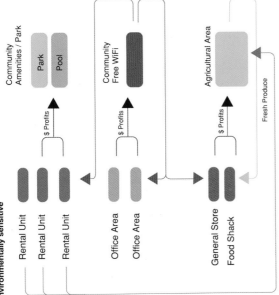

Hicksville, Long Island
Paradigmatic T.O.D

Three Distinct Zones emerge over time:

The Agricultural Network that will follow major auto oriented area, which would redevelop strip malls, gas stations and the like

The Transit Oriented Network which will follow the Station patterns and the regionally targeted parcels like the mall and big boxes

The Leftover areas of residential, which focus on minimizing extra car trips for basics

Long Island Rail Road
Major Automobile Roads
Transit Oriented Development Network (.5 walkability indicator)
Pooled Rental Income Stream Area
Big Box Redevelopment
Agricultural Corridor

Potential New Types

Neighborhood Feel   Downtown Feel

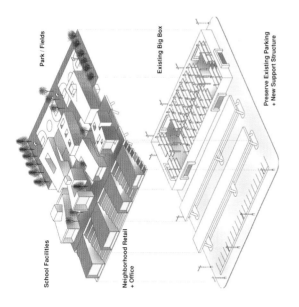

School Facilities

Park / Fields

Neighborhood Retail + Office

Existing Big Box

Preserve Existing Parking + New Support Structure

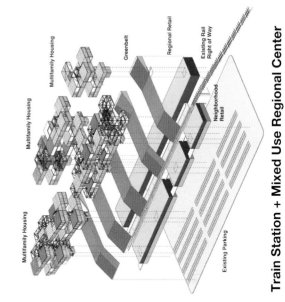

Big Box Retail + High School

Multifamily Housing

Greenbelt

Regional Retail

Existing Rail Right of Way

Neighborhood Retail

Existing Parking

Train Station + Mixed Use Regional Center

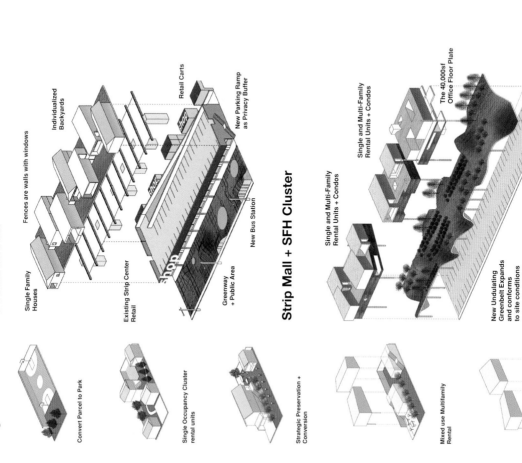

Single Family Houses

Fences are walls with windows

Individualized Backyards

Retail Carts

New Parking Ramp as Privacy Buffer

Existing Strip Center Retail

Greenway + Public Area

New Bus Station

Strip Mall + SFH Cluster

Single and Multi-Family Rental Units + Condos

Single and Multi-Family Rental Units + Condos

The 40,000sf Office Floor Plate

New Undulating Greenbelt Expands and conforms to site conditions

Existing Parking

Expanding Greenbelt + Stacked Mixed Use

Convert Parcel to Park

Single Occupancy Cluster rental units

Strategic Preservation + Conversion

Mixed use Multifamily Rental

Mixed use Multifamily Rental + SRO

AgIsland

Tom Jost (lead designer), Amy Ford-Wagner, Ebony Sterling, Philip Jonat, Emily Hull, Will Wagenlander, Meg Cederoth, Melanie George, David Greenblatt, and Melissa Targett (team) of Parsons Brinckerhoff

Summary

AgIsland suggests a new paradigm for relocating low-density, car-dependent commercial development to transit-served downtowns, thus replacing office parks with organic farms.

Themes

Retrofitting shopping centers and office parks, suburban agriculture, new mass transit networks, transit-oriented development (TOD), walkability, alternative energy production

Description

America's "first suburb" has long attracted families seeking open space, affordable home-ownership, local government and community. However, rapid automobile-oriented expansion has transformed this hamlet of farms and villages into a congested sprawl. Land is being gobbled up, taxes are skyrocketing, services are decreasing and communities are beginning to erode. Leaders are looking for solutions to generate new economies, improve the environment and restore the connection to local community.

Our proposal – AgIsland – envisions a new paradigm for economic, environmental and social development, combining the historic relationship of farming with new open space, decreased automobile dependence, alternative energy, a new economy and connection to the land and to each other. We have selected Farmingdale, along Route 110. Symbolic as a farm town replaced by millions of square feet of office parks, massive malls, strip centers and a few isolated residential developments, Farmingdale is a poster child for Long Island sprawl development.

AgIsland replaces office parks with organic farms, fed by AgTrain, a conveyer connected to processing, distribution and rail to connect all of Long Island to dense centers where goods are sold. AgTrain conveys waste to soil-mixing and waste-to-energy plants, providing organic soils to farms and alternative energy to the community.

The office parks are relocated to our transit-oriented community, served by LIRR and light rail on Route 110. Retail, education, entertainment and residential opportunities are mixed to significantly reduce automobile reliance. The result is an environmentally productive, socially diverse, eco-nomically industrious, livable, walkable community.

Jury comments

AgIsland looked to put the "farm" back in Farmingdale by proposing the replacement of office parks with organic farms.
– Allison Arieff

The strategy is simple: moving millions of square feet of office space currently located in isolated ex-urban office parks to the downtown and replacing them with local food production. . . . The entry offers a practical solution for the current detachment of urbanism and food production by creating a viable symbiosis between them.
– Galina Tachieva

The industrial enterprise that is "food," from production, to distribution, to point of sale, to its place on the dinner table, is likely one that most people take for granted. The power of the AgIsland entry is that it challenges, while at the same time demands, the viewer to conceptualize the complexity of the entire food process, and this is no easy task.
– Lee S. Sobel

AgIsland suggests a new kind of economy based on sustainable feed-back loops which use food, energy, and experience as a mode of exchange. If we are to survive the transition to a less fossil fuel dependent economy, innovative proposals that view community building as a comprehensive and integrated challenge are essential.
– Paul Lukez

Biography

Tom Jost, AICP, LEED-AP, is a senior urban strategist for the PlaceMaking group at the New York office of Parsons Brinckerhoff, a fourteen-thousand-person global infrastructure firm. His team of professionals provides a range of interrelated planning and design services for projects of all scales – from multijurisdictional policy planning to detailed streetscape and plaza design – using the link between transportation and land use as a catalyst for community revitalization and sustainable development. Previously, Jost managed the plan for the conversion of America's largest landfill, on Staten Island, into Freshkills Park, New York City's largest ecological habitat. He also managed the design and construction of NYC's High Line. A frequent lecturer, he is adjunct professor at Pratt Institute Graduate School of Architecture.

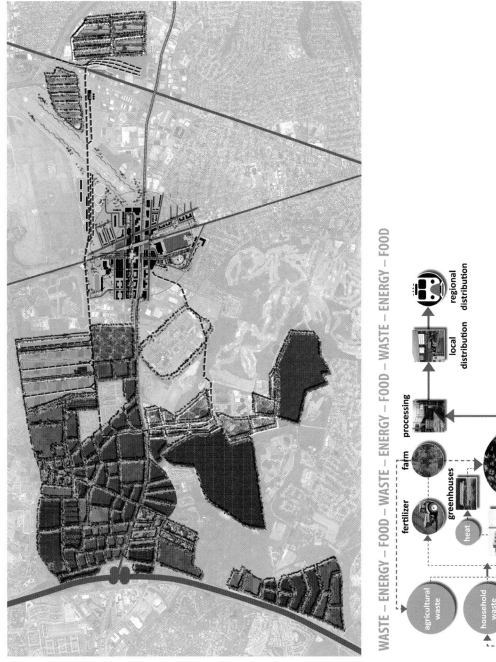

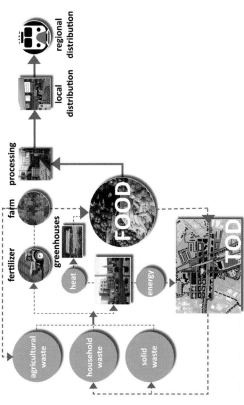

WASTE – ENERGY – FOOD – WASTE – ENERGY – FOOD – WASTE – ENERGY – FOOD

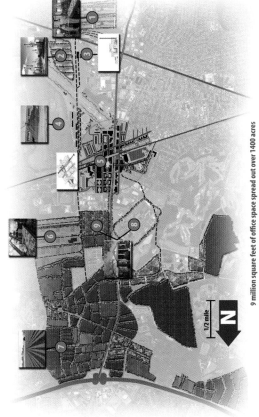

9 million square feet of office space spread out over 1400 acres **becomes**

1/2 mile

9 million square feet of office space spread out over 1,400 acres becomes 9 million square feet of office, new main street retail, condominiums, and single family residences on just 150 acres (throw in a museum, a public square, pedestrian streets, a greenmarket, 100 community farm plots, new parks, and mass transit connection to anywhere the LIRR goes.)

1. Food packaging and distribution center
2. Commercial greenhouses
3. Waste-to-energy plant
4. Soil-making center
5. Transit-oriented development (TOD)
6. Food processing centers
7. Organic farms
8. Farmingdale State University
9. Farmingdale A&T Extension

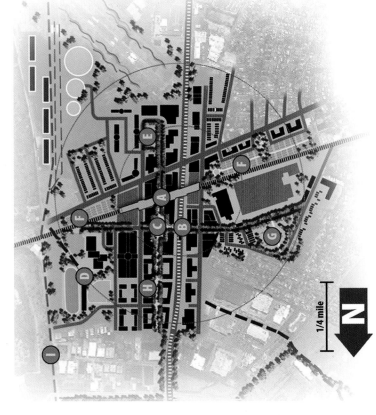

1/4 mile

AgIsland connects food to waste to energy in a closed loop, sharing the outputs of each component to mutual advantage to create a community independent of fossil fuels, independent of automobiles, and connected to healthy organic food, open space, and the varied lifestyle choices that attract people to urban destinations.

– Electricity for 5,000 households generated from waste

– 46,000 tons of garbage diverted from landfills annually

– Replaces need for 4,000 gallons of fuel a day

– 1,400 acres of new agricultural space preserved

– 7,500 tons of organic crops grown annually (5,600 people)

– Upwards of 20,000 daily auto trips diverted

A. LIRR Republic Station
B. Route 10 light rail
C. Central Plaza
D. Magnet High School
E. Farmers market
F. Community gardens
G. Community park
H. Pedestrian street
I. AgTrain

Long Island has succumbed to automobile/sprawl infrastructure, its pastoral landscape reduced to an endless horizon of strip centers – choking on congestion, losing its business and its residents, and looking ahead to higher costs and more time spent in traffic. What can this great suburb do to stimulate new growth, reduce congestion, create new open space and new energy sources, and build new communities where we can maintain balance among our economic, social and environmental needs?

AgIsland proposes a new paradigm for suburban growth, combining farming with transit-oriented development.

– Decrease automobile dependency
– Develop new opportunities for employment and growth
– Sustain the economy
– Lower the carbon foorprint
– Create healthy livable comminties

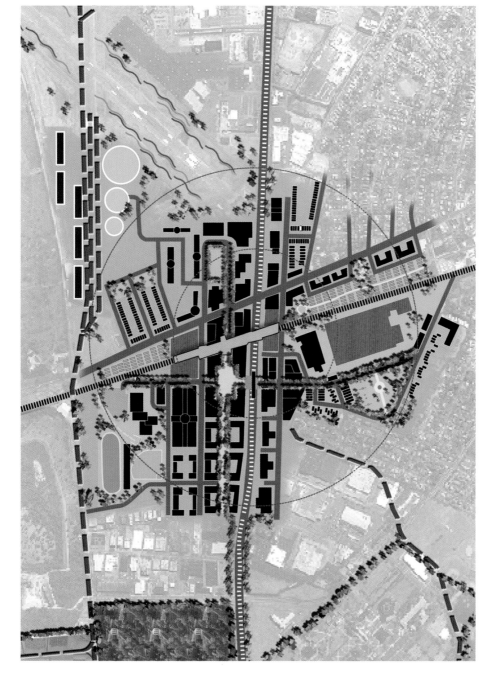

Building C-Burbia
Denise Hoffman Brandt with Alexa Helsell and Bronwyn Gropp

Summary

C-Burbia is a landscape proposition at multiple scales for addressing climate change with an exciting new kind of infrastructure designed to efficiently sequester carbon in plantings.

Themes

Ecological repair, landscape improvements, retrofitting auto infrastructure, suburban agriculture

Description

"Building C-Burbia" – the C stands for carbon – is an infrastructure system for short-term biomass storage and formation of long-term soil carbon reservoirs in suburban landscape. As the northeast metropolitan regions anticipate remediation of anthropogenic climate change – and policy-makers navigate the land-ethics of disproportionate responsibility for negative global impacts – mandates that assure existing infrastructures comply with updated environmental standards must be complemented by implementation of new infrastructures that redress failures of the old systems. Cap and trade and the United Nations Intergovernmental Panel on Climate Change (IPCC) protocols are emerging to adapt to the need for new environmental paradigms. In the post-carbon world, design and planning initiatives must be systemically integrated, yet opportunistic, to achieve efficiency. The C-Burbia system was designed to disperse across the urban field, latching onto existing physical structures, policy, and funding mechanisms to optimize carbon cycle performance and amplify the experiential intensity of suburban landscape.

Opportunistic infill with carbon sink infrastructure leverages a proactive response to global climate change to instigate densification of suburban morphology. Suburban development is squeezed in a positive way – "hugged" as it were – by the new infrastructural zones, which themselves generate desirable conditions to draw out a younger population of new ecological suburbanites. Metrics for the new systems are evolving; a key aspect of the C-Burbia study was the objective to delineate a systemic approach to environmental infrastructure. Individually, each sink benefits its context with multiple functions: storm water management, habitat improvement, human ecological education, and more compelling local experiential qualities of the place. Expanding the suburban-plant typology to encompass evolving plant communities and productive plantations activates terrestrial soil sequestration across a spectrum of effective time frames.

Jury comments

I really admire the combined pragmatism and ambition of this project. C-Burbia works with the sidewalks, medians, and other underutilized land to mitigate and remediate the suburban landscape.
– Georgeen Theodore

This is one of the most complex and comprehensive proposals, thoroughly researched, richly illustrated, and acknowledging the relationship between sprawl development and climate change. The project is centered on ecological infrastructure for carbon sequestration in the form of green easements and swales, pervious surfaces, larger plots for urban agriculture, replacing asphalt, high-maintenance lawns, and underutilized spaces.
– Galina Tachieva

This team developed creative yet viable strategies for sequestering carbon while generating a kind of utopian landscape in suburbia.
– Paul Lukez

Biographies

Denise Hoffman Brandt, RLA, is principal of Hoffman Brandt Projects LLC and director of landscape architecture at the Spitzer School of Architecture at the City College of New York. She was a New York Prize Fellow of the Van Alen Institute's Projects in Public Architecture program, where she developed the project "City Sink," recipient of an Environmental Design Research Association Great Places Research Award and published in a book of the same title.

Alexa Helsell is a landscape designer at Hewitt in Seattle. She received an MLA from the City College of New York, where she received a Spitzer Travel Scholarship to support research on the Tiber River in Rome.

Bronwyn Gropp is a landscape designer at Robin Key Landscape Architecture in New York. She received an MLA from the City College of New York and was awarded a Thesis Prize.

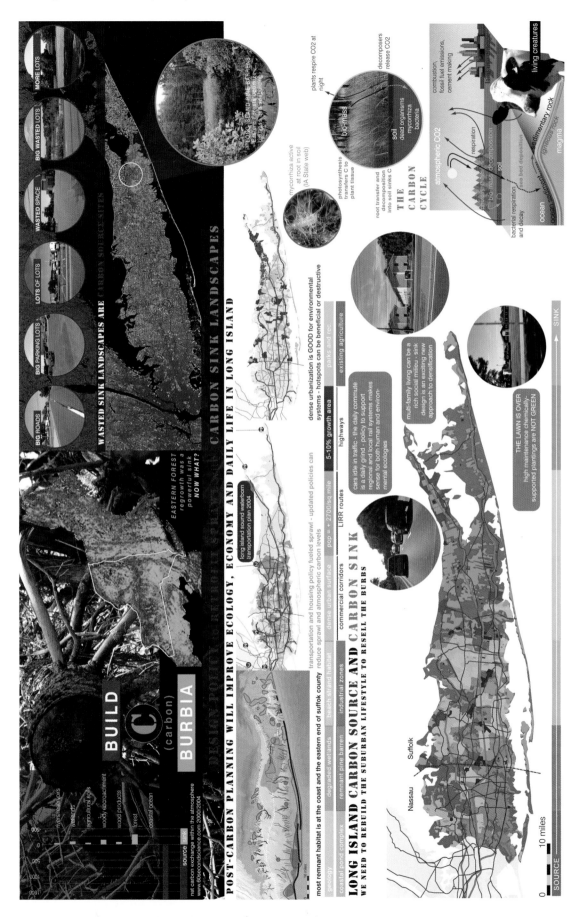

POST-CARBON PLANNING WILL IMPROVE ECOLOGY, ECONOMY AND DAILY LIFE IN LONG ISLAND

CARBON SINK LANDSCAPES

WASTED SINK LANDSCAPES ARE CARBON SOURCE SITES

MORE LOTS | BIG WASTED LOTS | WASTED SPACE | LOTS OF LOTS | BIG PARKING LOTS | BIG ROADS

DESIGN POTENT: REBUILD SPRAWL as a CARBON SINK

BUILD
C
(carbon)
BURBIA

EASTERN FOREST
regrowth was a
powerful sink
NOW WHAT?

source | sink
net carbon exchange within the atmosphere
www.60secondscience.com 2000/2004

rivers/transports
wetlands
agricultural soils
woody encroachment
wood products
forest
coastal ocean

LONG ISLAND CARBON SOURCE AND CARBON SINK
WE NEED TO REBUILD THE SUBURBAN LIFESTYLE TO RESELL THE BURBS

most remnant habitat is at the coast and the eastern end of suffolk county

transportation and housing policy fueled sprawl - updated policies can
reduce sprawl and atmospheric carbon levels

ecology | coastal pond complex | degraded wetlands | remnant pine barren | beach strand habitat | industrial zones | dense urban surface | commercial corridors | 5-10% growth area | parks and rec | existing agriculture

pop = 2700/sq.mile

LIRR routes | highways

long island sound waterborn
transportation plan 2004

dense urbanization is GOOD for environmental
systems - hotspots can be beneficial or destructive

cars idle in traffic - the daily commute
is a daily grind - policy to support
regional and local rail systems makes
sense for both human and environmental ecologies

multi-family living can be a
rich social milieu - sink
design is an exciting new
approach to densification

THE LAWN IS OVER
high maintenance chemically-
supported plantings are NOT GREEN

Nassau | Suffolk

0 | 10 miles

SOURCE | SINK

THE CARBON CYCLE

atmospheric CO2

respiration

combustion,
fossil fuel emissions,
cement making

living creatures

land use change

sedimentary rock
igneous rock
magma

ocean sediments

soil

bio-mass
sea bed deposition
bacterial respiration
and decay

decomposition

plants respire CO2 at
night

decomposers
release CO2

soil
bio-mass
dead organisms
mycorrhiza
bacteria

photosynthesis
transfers C to
plant tissue

root transfer and
decomposition
into soil sinks C

mycorrhiza active
at root in soil
(IA State web)

LONG ISLAND PINE BARRENS
Eastern Forest soils and
biomass are still building

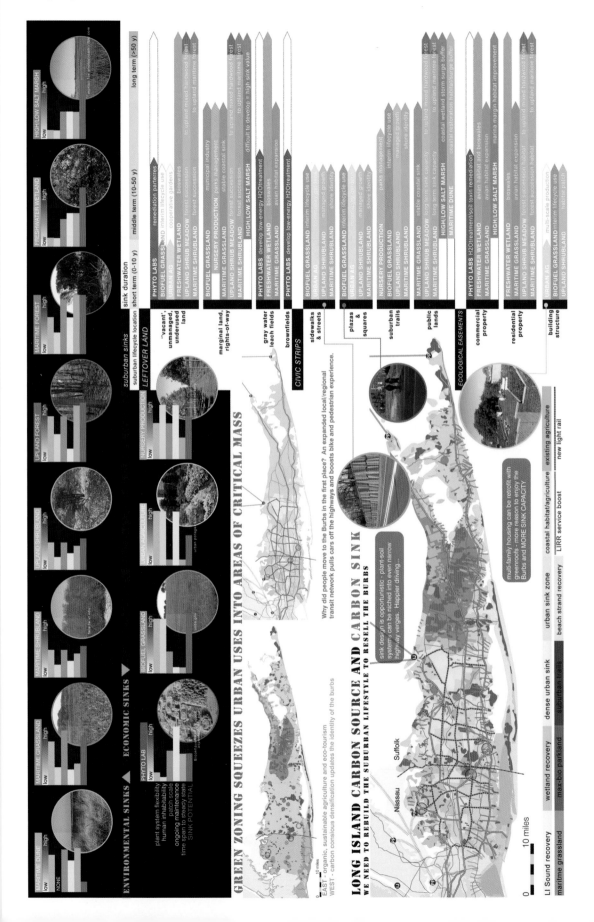

GREEN ZONING SQUEEZES URBAN USES INTO AREAS OF CRITICAL MASS

EAST - organic, sustainable agriculture and eco-tourism
WEST - carbon conscious densification updates the identity of the burbs

LONG ISLAND CARBON SOURCE AND CARBON SINK
WE NEED TO REBUILD THE SUBURBAN LIFESTYLE TO RESELL THE BURBS

CIVIC 'STRIPS' STRIPS ADD UP - EVEN A NARROW TEN FOOT WIDE BAND PROVIDES AN ACRE OF RESOURCE LAND IN 8 MILES

GLEN COVE

FARMINGDALE

BABYLON

EXISTING ROAD

NO LONGER A WASTELAND

I'D RATHER TAKE THE TRAIN

nursery production
maritime forest
urban agriculture
phyto-labs
biofuel grassland
high and low salt marsh
freshwater wetland
maritime dune
maritime grassland
upland forest
maritime shrubland

LIGHT RAIL WITH SINK SURFACE

CIVIC STRIPS: boosting the identity of commerical corridors and creating new civic places animated with plant-soil systems can be supported by cross-funding opportunities. Transportation, environmental, energy, community-building, technology, waste management and commerce funding can be operationalized depending on the flexibility of the proposal. These new public projects will redefine the character of the increasingly dense urban zones.

ROAD RETROFIT - New bioswales and biofuel grasslands animate wide roads. Cars are squeezed encouraging public transit use.

ECOLOGICAL EASEMENTS: RETROFITTING SPRAWL SPACE WITH ECOLOGICAL INFRASTRUCTURE FOR CARBON STORAGE

GLEN COVE

FARMINGDALE

BABYLON

EXISTING ROAD

WELCOME TO THE C-BURBS

NEXT TIME I'LL TAKE THE TRAIN

nursery / graduation
maritime forest
phyto-labs
high and low salt marsh
biofuel grassland
freshwater wetland
upland forest
maritime shrubland
maritime dune
maritime grassland

0   1000 feet

PHYTO-REMEDIATION LABS CAN BE BEAUTIFUL

ECOLOGICAL EASEMENTS: are a mechanism for creation of community space. Like most easements, established to facilitate infrastructural operations, sink easements open zones for an overlay of ecological services within large-scale suburban morphology.

5'   8' bikeway   5'   28' grass paver   20'   5'   6'

1   3   5   10

LOTS MATTER - New bioswales and grass-crete bikeways encroach on excess asphalt. Slow residential drives are all pervious. Glen Cove's storm water overflow is radically decreased - leading to higher oxygen levels in the Sound

LEFTOVER LAND: SINK TYPES ARE SYNCHRONIZED TO SUBURBAN LAND USE LIFE-CYCLES

GLEN COVE

FARMINGDALE

BABYLON

Urban agriculture doesn't have to be scrappy gardens, rather it is a collective organization of interim use production, green parking and native grassland, placeholders until development pressure in more constrained areas stimulates growth. (white outlines)

nursery production
urban agriculture
maritime forest
phyto-labs
biofuel grassland
high and low salt marsh
freshwater wetland
maritime dune
maritime grassland
upland forest
maritime shrubland

0 1000 feet

VACANT/UNMANAGED/UNDERUSED LOTS: these properties are passive zones, either inactive or inert, they present opportunities for various sink activation time-scales. Stable zones, leach fields, right-of-ways and brownfields for example, can be operationalized for longer term storage in sync with remediation processes. Vacant lots and other land subject to short-term use change and market forces can be operationalized for cycling biomass carbon storage as an ecological-economic initiative.

OUT FOR A WALK ON THE SUBURBAN TRAILS

THE TOWN MAKES THE CALL

instant

incremental

SUBHUB Transit System

Michael Piper and Frank Ruchala of DUB Studios

Summary

SUBHUB proposes a feeder transit system, in-triguingly anchored at public school sites, both reducing commuter car storage in downtowns and providing enhanced civic hubs in surrounding neighborhoods.

Themes

New mass transit networks, new uses for schools, strengthening the public/civic realm, supporting local economies

Description

Connecting town center train stations to their outlying suburbs, SUBHUB is a micro-infrastructure scaled for a more walkable, industrious and active suburbia. The system has three parts: re-imagined transit, a HUB at existing train stations, and SUBHUBs at existing public schools.

Transit

Too big for suburbia, existing transit is down-sized and multiplied to cover more ground. To pay the cost of the expanded system, SUBHUB combines transit with other public services and product delivery.

HUB

At the existing train station, trains exchange passengers and freight with a smaller shuttle system that extends through the suburbs. Additionally, combining freight with passenger transit provides an affordable way for small-scale businesses to ship goods.

SUBHUB

In addition to making transit stops and public space at school sites in suburbia, SUBHUB provides a right-sized system for getting home-grown vegetables and products to market. Collectively the component pieces provide a means for acting on town centers and sprawling suburbs alike. After all, the city is more than its center alone.

Jury comments

The dissipative development patterns found in suburbia are countered in this proposal. Intensely developed "subhubs" connected by newly integrated low-cost transportation systems allow for a new suburban fabric to be generated, one offering a better and more sustainable quality of life.
– Paul Lukez

The jurors appreciated the connection to schools – an imperfect but intriguing way to address how few kids walk to schools these days – and the attention to seldom-addressed issues like food miles traveled.
– Allison Arieff

This project displays unconventional thinking about connectivity and the new economic synergies in suburbia. The transit stations become small-business generators with markets, freight exchange and cart rentals, while the school sites are infilled with efficient new buildings to create centers for the surrounding communities.
– Galina Tachieva

This submission is a clever, well-presented value-added response to the problem of intra-suburban transportation. Its aim – improving intra-suburban transportation and leveraging the investment for an improved public realm – is laudable.
– Daniel D'Oca

This project acts like a parasite on the suburb's infrastructure; however, rather than weakening its host, the result is all sorts of new forms of public life.
– Georgeen Theodore

Bold colors, a simple layout, and easy to under-stand characters and symbols, combine to create images that add strength to SUBHUB's message. It is important not to forget how powerful the use of good visual design can be when communicating concepts and ideas.
– Lee S. Sobel

Biographies

Michael Piper is a co-founder of DUB Studios, a small firm engaged in speculative urban projects and commissioned projects at a range of scales. He has taught architecture and urban design at Columbia, Harvard, Syracuse, the City College of New York, and Ohio State University, where he was a Lefevre Fellow. He received his MArch from Harvard and BS in architecture from Georgia Tech.

Frank Ruchala Jr. is an associate urban planner and designer in the New York Department of City Planning's Manhattan Office, where he is project manager for Midtown and Hudson Yards. He is engaged in ongoing research on the impact of oil fields on the development of the Los Angeles region, published in *The Infrastructural City: Networked Ecologies in Los Angeles* (2008). He teaches in the urban design program at Columbia. He received his MArch from Harvard and BA from Rutgers.

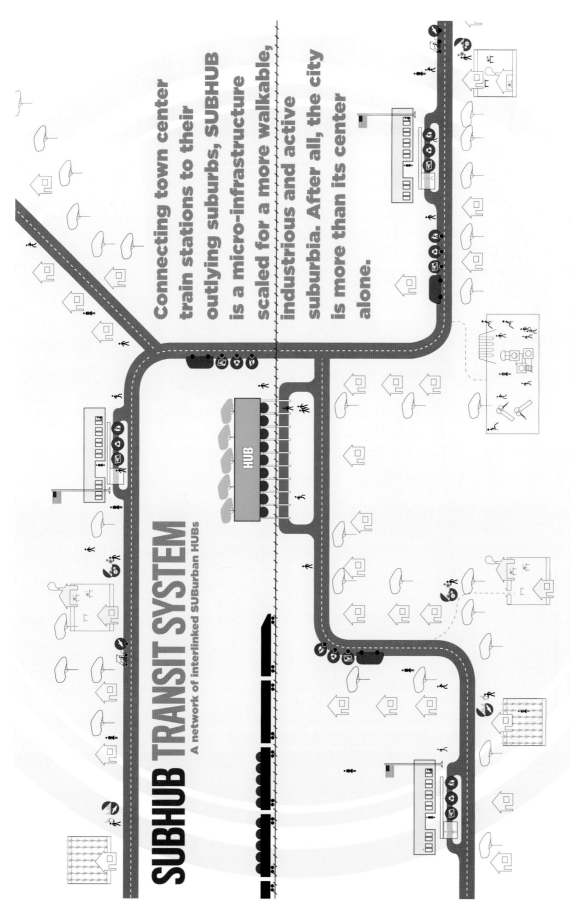

SUBHUB TRANSIT SYSTEM
A network of interlinked SUBurban HUBs

Connecting town center train stations to their outlying suburbs, SUBHUB is a micro-infrastructure scaled for a more walkable, industrious and active suburbia. After all, the city is more than its center alone.

HUB

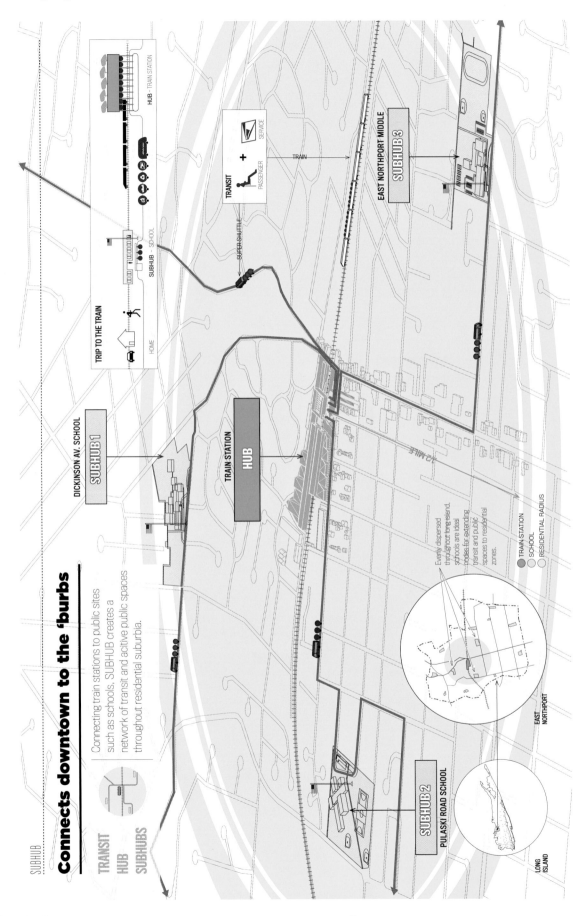

SUBHUB

Connects downtown to the 'burbs

Connecting train stations to public sites such as schools. SUBHUB creates a network of transit and active public spaces throughout residential suburbia.

TRANSIT
HUB
SUBHUBS

TRIP TO THE TRAIN

HOME

SUBHUB - SCHOOL

HUB - TRAIN STATION

TRANSIT

PASSENGER + SERVICE

SUPER SHUTTLE

TRAIN

DICKINSON AV. SCHOOL

SUBHUB 1

TRAIN STATION

HUB

EAST NORTHPORT MIDDLE

SUBHUB 3

½ MILE

Evenly dispersed throughout Long Island, schools are ideal nodes for extending transit and public spaces to residential zones.

TRAIN STATION
SCHOOL
RESIDENTIAL RADIUS

EAST NORTHPORT

SUBHUB 2

PULASKI ROAD SCHOOL

LONG ISLAND

SUBHUB

Consolidates to cover more ground

To big for suburbia, existing transit is downsized and multiplied to cover more ground. To pay the cost of the expanded system, SUBHUB combines transit with other public services and product delivery.

TRANSIT
HUB
SUBHUBS

SUPER SHUTTLE

SUBHUB SCALES DOWN BUSES TO COVER THE SUBURBS BETTER. COMBINING TRANSIT AND SERVICES TO MAKE DOWNSIZING THEM AFFORDABLE.

TRAIN

TRAINS RUN UNDER CAPACITY AT MID DAY. SUBHUB USES LEFT OVER SPACE TO SHIP GOODS AND SERVICES.

SUBHUB

Builds small business beside transit stations

TRANSIT
HUB
SUBHUBS

Reintroducing freight to passenger rail, SUBHUB facilitates small industry next to train stations. Combining freight with transit provides an affordable way for small scale businesses to ship goods.

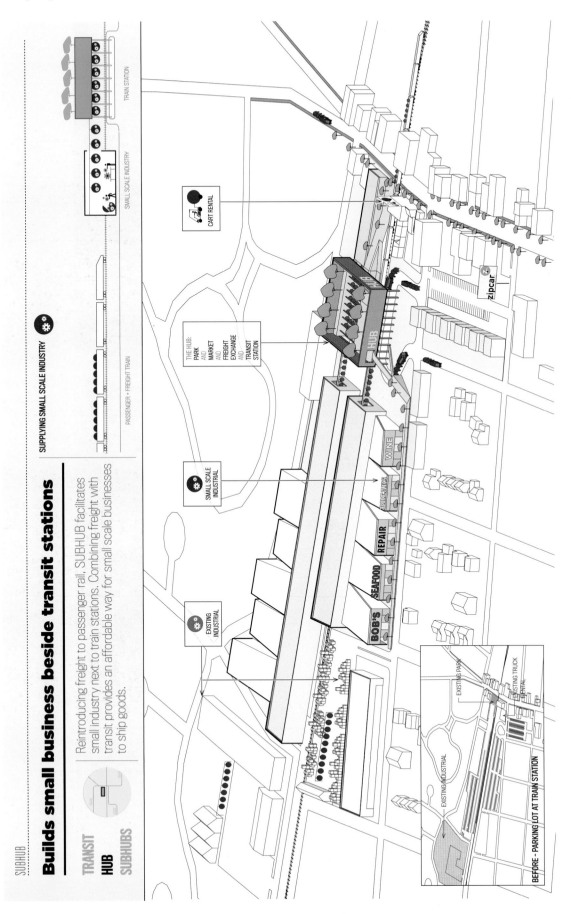

SUPPLYING SMALL SCALE INDUSTRY

TRAIN STATION

SMALL SCALE INDUSTRY

PASSENGER + FREIGHT TRAIN

CART RENTAL

zipcar

THE HUB: PARK AND MARKET AND FREIGHT EXCHANGE AND TRANSIT STATION

HUB

SMALL SCALE INDUSTRIAL

EXISTING INDUSTRIAL

WINE

BREWERY

REPAIR

SEAFOOD

BOB'S

EXISTING INDUSTRIAL

EXISTING PARK

EXISTING TRUCK RENTAL

BEFORE - PARKING LOT AT TRAIN STATION

91

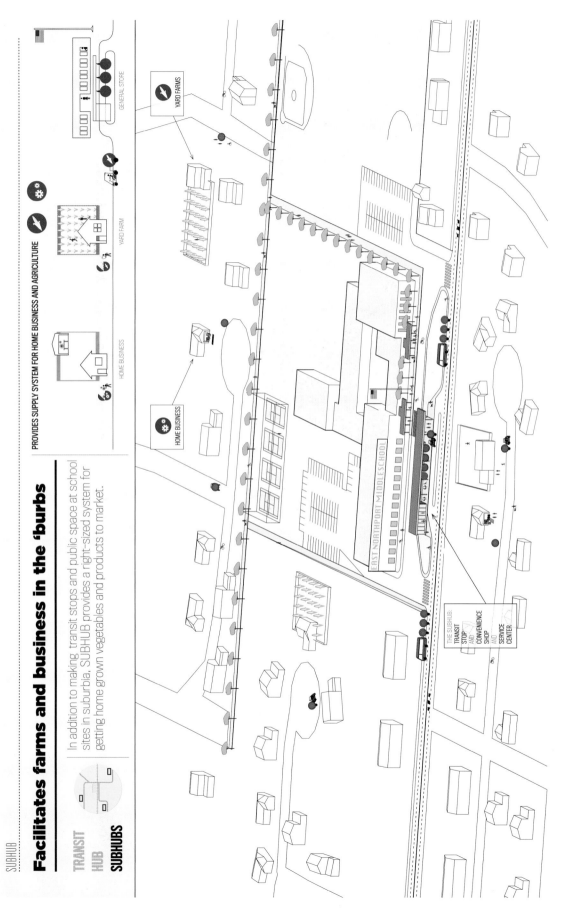

SUBHUB

Facilitates farms and business in the 'burbs

TRANSIT HUB SUBHUBS

In addition to making transit stops and public space at school sites in suburbia, SUBHUB provides a right-sized system for getting home grown vegetables and products to market.

PROVIDES SUPPLY SYSTEM FOR HOME BUSINESS AND AGRICULTURE

GENERAL STORE

YARD FARM

HOME BUSINESS

YARD FARMS

HOME BUSINESS

EAST NORTHPORT MIDDLE SCHOOL

THE SUBHUB:
TRANSIT STOP AND CONVENIENCE SHOP AND SERVICE CENTER

Long Division

Network Architecture Lab (Kazys Varnelis, director; Leigha Dennis, Momo Araki, Alexis Burson, and Kyle Hovenkotter) and PARC Office (William Prince)

Summary

Long Division emphasizes the dire need to conserve freshwater resources, provocatively suggesting that only some downtowns should grow into dense and diverse centers, while others might shrink, that is depopulate, over time.

Themes

Ecological repair, innovative building types, infill development, supporting social diversity, transforming zoning

Description

Long Division is a regional planning strategy embracing both voiding and densification based on the needs of the local population and geography.

Suburban redevelopment must be regional. Our proposal divides Long Island into two zones based on infrastructural and ecological factors: Western Long Island is already relatively dense, integrated into the metropolitan area by rail, while eastern Long Island is underserved by infrastructure. Moreover, Long Island sits on one of the most productive aquifers in the country and needs to defend this to assure its future.

To this end, we propose no-growth zones for the east and north where the aquifer is deepest and closest to the surface. As the population of that area ages, communities such as Riverhead revert to dense villages surrounded by sustainable farming, nature preserves and other uses compatible with aquifer preservation while serving as an amenity for the vacation region of the Hamptons and for the dense west.

In the west, we propose a second-city approach, creating a viable set of dense centers both as a support area for New York and also as independent, productive communities. Typologies aim to increase diversity between communities and create identity rather than homogeneity in downtowns. Instead of searching for one solution, we propose a set of solutions for housing, open space, and productivity, each responding to an area's population: e.g., seniors, aspiring minorities, recent immigrants, and artists/artisans. Over time, outlying areas within suburbs will become voided to serve as buffers that sustain community identity.

Jury comments

Long Division, concerned about the contamination of Long Island's aquifers, aims to establish a regional strategy to promote both growth and contraction. Proposing alternatives to conventional single-family housing... is an important strategy for developing more sustainable approaches to sprawl.
– Allison Arieff

The proposal offers a range of buildings and public spaces for infill, presented in clever combinations of mixed uses: elderly housing with a botanical garden, a train station with bike storage, shared office workshops with a communal space.
– Galina Tachieva

I appreciated the regional scale of this proposal. Long Division pragmatically acknowledges that there are always winners and losers in every planning project.
– Georgeen Theodore

Biographies

Directed by Kazys Varnelis, the Network Architecture Lab is a think tank at the Columbia University Graduate School of Architecture, Planning, and Preservation that investigates the impact of telecommunication, digital technology, and changing social demographics on architecture, urbanism, and society. Varnelis, also a faculty member at the University of Limerick, Ireland, received his PhD in the history of architecture and urban development from Cornell and is author and editor of numerous publications.

William Prince, RA, AICP, LEED BD+C, is principal and founder of Planning Architecture Research Curatorial (PARC) Office in New York. Recently completed projects include the Gucci Museum in Florence and the Le Meridien Etiler Hotel & Residences in Istanbul. Before founding his own firm, Prince worked for the Rockwell Group, OMA, Rogers Marvel, and Bernard Tschumi. Prince currently teaches architecture studio at Parsons the New School for Design. He received his MArch from Harvard and BArch from the Ohio State University.

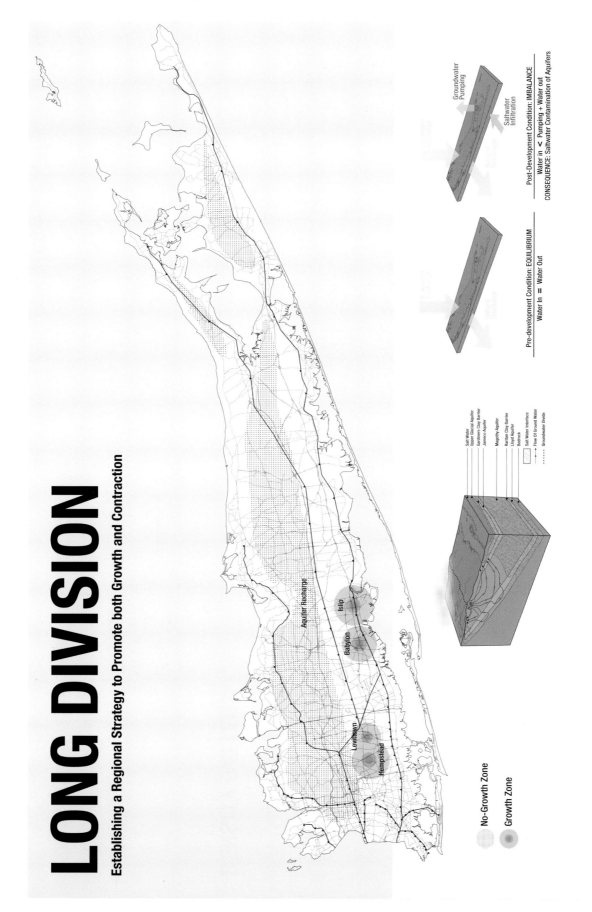

LONG DIVISION

Establishing a Regional Strategy to Promote both Growth and Contraction

Aquifer Recharge

Islip

Babylon

Levittown

Hempstead

Groundwater Pumping

Saltwater Infiltration

Post-Development Condition: IMBALANCE
Water in < Pumping + Water out
CONSEQUENCE: Saltwater Contamination of Aquifers

Pre-development Condition: EQUILIBRIUM
Water In = Water Out

Salt Water
Upper Glacial Aquifer
Gardiners Clay Barrier
Jameco Aquifer
Magothy Aquifer
Raritan Clay Barrier
Lloyd Aquifer
Bedrock
Salt Water Interface
Flow Of Ground Water
Groundwater Divide

No-Growth Zone

Growth Zone

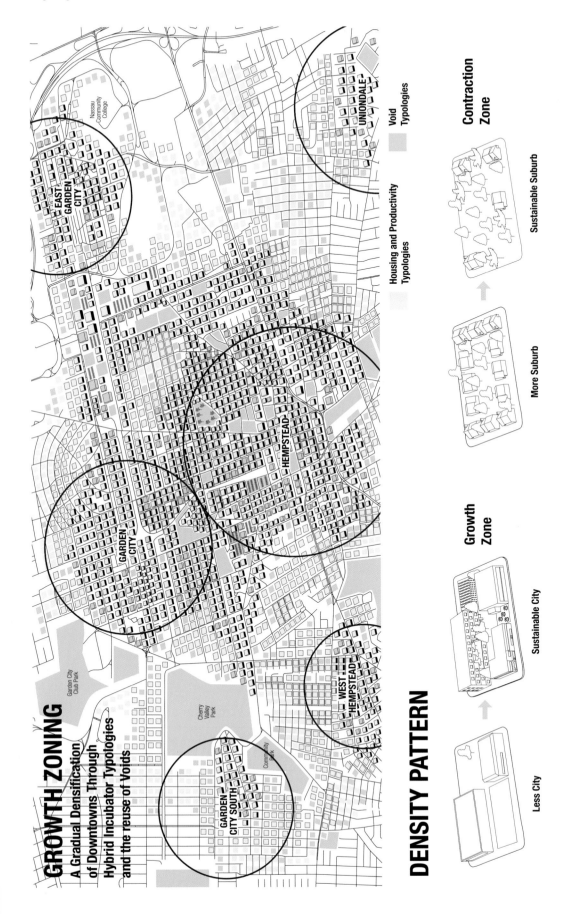

GROWTH ZONING

A Gradual Densification of Downtowns Through Hybrid Incubator Typologies and the reuse of Voids

Void Typologies

Housing and Productivity Typologies

DENSITY PATTERN

Less City

Sustainable City

Growth Zone

More Suburb

Sustainable Suburb

Contraction Zone

GENERATIVE TYPOLOGIES

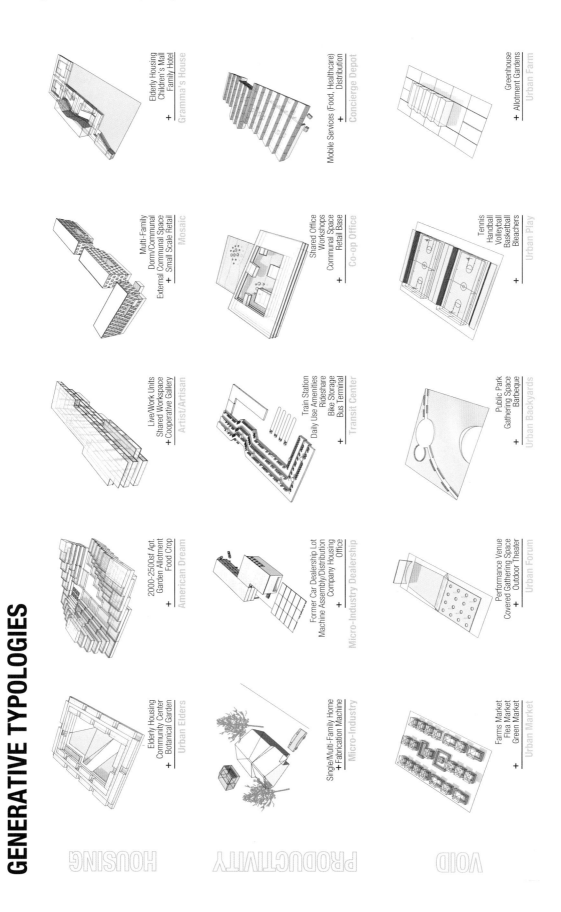

Elderly Housing
Children's Mall
Family Hotel
+
Gramma's House

Mobile Services (Food, Healthcare)
Distribution
+
Concierge Depot

Greenhouse
+ Allotment Gardens
Urban Farm

Multi-Family
Dorm/Communal
External Communal Space
+ Small Scale Retail
Mosaic

Shared Office
Workshops
Communal Space
Retail Base
+
Co-op Office

Tennis
Handball
Volleyball
Basketball
Bleachers
+
Urban Play

Live/Work Units
Shared Workspace
+ Cooperative Gallery
Artist/Artisan

Train Station
Daily Use Amenities
Rideshare
Bike Storage
Bus Terminal
+
Transit Center

Public Park
Gathering Space
Barbeque
+
Urban Backyards

2000-2500sf Apt.
Garden Allotment
Food Crop
+
American Dream

Former Car Dealership Lot
Machine Assembly/Distribution
Company Housing
Office
+
Micro-Industry Dealership

Performance Venue
Covered Gathering Space
Outdoor Theater
+
Urban Forum

Elderly Housing
Community Center
Botanical Garden
+
Urban Elders

Single/Multi-Family Home
+ Fabrication Machine
Micro-Industry

Farms Market
Flea Market
Green Market
+
Urban Market

HOUSING

PRODUCTIVITY

VOID

HEMPSTEAD: INSTANT CITY

HEMPSTEAD: INSTANT CITY

Columbia Ave. looking west from Hempstead Train Station

LIRR: Long Island Radically Rezoned
Tobias Holler, Katelyn Mulry, Sven Peters, and Ana Serra

Summary

A radical island-wide reorganization of regional governance structure for a carbon-neutral future comprised of a network of dense centers with agricultural and open space in between.

Themes

Transforming zoning, alternative energy production, suburban agriculture, ecological repair, retrofitting shopping centers, multiunit housing

Description

What if we draw on the metabolism of an island to provide a regenerative natural environment? What if we push innovation and create synergies between the various resource streams to arrive at systemic solutions? We then have a Living Island proposal, applying closed loop principles on a macro scale: water, energy and waste neutral and 100% local food production. In order to share resources efficiently the current administrative structure is eliminated in favor of a "proximity-to-mass-transit" (LIRR) based structure: the Smart Cells – polygons which have infrastructure as the driver and a natural perimeter: a restorative connective fabric for habitat, recreation and agriculture, a 50/50 balance between nature and man-made.

To obtain the area needed we capitalize on the densification potential of the downtowns. Four strategies are applied to revitalize and repopulate these vacant and lifeless areas:

Fix-a-Block

"Wrap" blocks given over to surface parking with public program/retail around existing buildings and over parking structures and add low-rise high density residential "carpet" on top.

Re-Center

Create central public space at the train station; this new vibrant downtown center is an extension of the eco-boulevard and re-centers towns to give them a new identity where a folded landscape of public space bridges from street level to elevated train tracks.

Mall Chopper

Subdivide large underutilized surface parking around mall into small blocks that echo the small-scale grain of the surrounding context. Apply fix-a-block rules.

Resi-Dense

Densify residential fabric by inserting additional units around existing single-family houses.

Jury comments

This project envisions a radical reshuffling of land uses and densities to address some of the more vexing problems facing suburbia. The imageability is strong.

– Georgeen Theodore

Biographies

Tobias Holler, AIA, LEED AP, is the principal of HOLLER architecture, an award-winning research and design practice in Brooklyn, New York. He is an assistant professor of architecture at the New York Institute of Technology. He received an MArch from Pratt Institute in Brooklyn, where he was a Fulbright Scholar in 2003.

Katelyn Mulry received a BArch from the New York Institute of Technology and is currently a graduate student at the University of Pennsylvania School of Design.

Sven Peters is the principal of Brooklyn-based Atelier Sven Peters. He received an MArch from Pratt Institute in Brooklyn, where he was a Fulbright Scholar in 2004.

Ana Serra, LEED AP, is an associate sustainability consultant at Buro Happold Consulting Engineers in New York City. She received a BArch from the New York Institute of Technology and an MS in environmental design and engineering from The Bartlett, University of London.

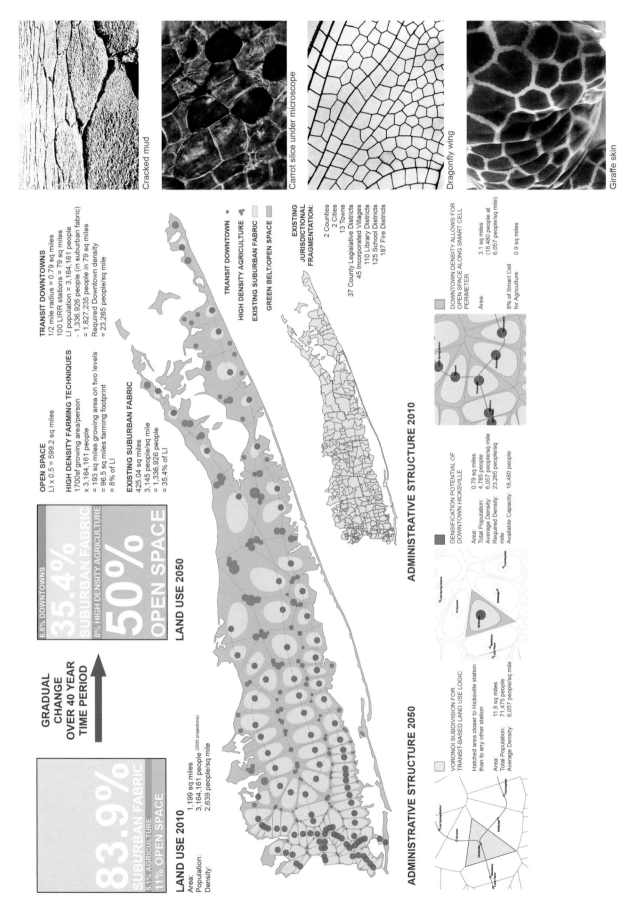

Cracked mud

Carrot slice under microscope

Dragonfly wing

Giraffe skin

GRADUAL CHANGE OVER 40 YEAR TIME PERIOD

83.9% SUBURBAN FABRIC
5.1% AGRICULTURE
11% OPEN SPACE

LAND USE 2010
Area: 1,199 sq miles
Population: 3,164,161 people (2030 projections)
Density: 2,639 people/sq mile

6.6% DOWNTOWNS
35.4% SUBURBAN FABRIC
8% HIGH DENSITY AGRICULTURE
50% OPEN SPACE

LAND USE 2050

OPEN SPACE
LI x 0.5 = 599.2 sq miles

HIGH DENSITY FARMING TECHNIQUES
1700sf growing area/person
x 3,164,161 people
= 193 sq miles growing area on two levels
= 96.5 sq miles farming footprint
= 8% of LI

EXISTING SUBURBAN FABRIC
425.04 sq miles
3,145 people/sq mile
= 1,336,926 people
= 35.4% of LI

TRANSIT DOWNTOWNS
1/2 mile radius = 0.79 sq miles
100 LIRR stations = 79 sq miles
- 1,336,926 people (in suburban fabric)
LI population = 3,164,161 people
= 1,827,235 people in 79 sq miles
Required Downtown density
= 23,265 people/sq mile

TRANSIT DOWNTOWN ·
HIGH DENSITY AGRICULTURE
EXISTING SUBURBAN FABRIC
GREEN BELT/OPEN SPACE

EXISTING JURISDICTIONAL FRAGMENTATION:
2 Counties
2 Cities
13 Towns
37 County Legislative Districts
45 Incorporated Villages
110 Library Districts
125 School Districts
187 Fire Districts

ADMINISTRATIVE STRUCTURE 2010

ADMINISTRATIVE STRUCTURE 2050

VORONOI SUBDIVISION FOR TRANSIT-BASED LAND USE LOGIC

Hatched area closer to Hicksville station than to any other station

Area: 11.8 sq miles
Total Population: 71,475 people
Average Density: 6,057 people/sq mile

DENSIFICATION POTENTIAL OF DOWNTOWN HICKSVILLE

Area: 0.79 sq miles
Total Population: 4,785 people
Average Density: 6,057 people/sq mile
Required Density: 23,265 people/sq mile
Available Capacity: 18,480 people

DOWNTOWN DENSITY ALLOWS FOR OPEN SPACE ALONG SMART CELL PERIMETER

Area: 3.1 sq miles (18,480 people at 6,057 people/sq miles)

8% of Smart Cell for Agriculture: 0.9 sq miles

restored 'Hempstead Plains' grassland, the native prairie habitat of western Long Island

former road turned into linear park

GREEN BELT
A Green Belt is created where the 'kidneys' that support the smart cells are found. Waste processing and treatment, water treatment energy plants and agriculture are all located here. The remainder of the green belt is dedicated to nature and habitat restoration, in essence a carbon sink, but also the 'lungs' of Long Island.

restored atlantic coastal pine barren ecosystem

constructed wetland within footprint of former suburban homes

EXISTING LIRR COMMUTER RAIL
Regional East-West connectivity

BOULEVARDS W/ LIGHT RAIL
Retrofitting highway infrastructure for regional North-South connectivity

HYBRID BUSES
Connecting remaining suburban areas to the transit downtowns

LONG ISLAND BIKEWAY

INTERMODAL NODE

TRANSIT DOWNTOWNS
Restricted car access zone

RECREATIONAL PROGRAM
Along edge of suburban fabric

RENATURALIZED AREAS & HABITAT RESTORATION

HIGH EFFICIENCY AGRICULTURE

BALANCE OF NATURE & MAN-MADE

100% RENEWABLE ENERGY

100% WATER NEUTRAL

100% LOCAL FOOD

0% WASTE TO LANDFILL

PROJECT DESCRIPTION
The essence of sustainability is based on the principles of using resources efficiently in a way that they can replenish themselves. In order to attain sustainability, existing 'boundaries', of all sorts, and the restrictions that they impose, must be removed.

The sharing of resources, the 'Scale Jumping' principle from the Living Building Challenge framework, becomes a vital necessity, as recognized by the LBC.

In our proposal we investigated the potential for Long Island in NY, currently comprised of 117 towns, to become a single urban system entity, functioning as a city of 2.7 habitants, to be self sufficient and LBC compliant. Through Radical Rezoning, this self contained system, when looked at holistically, has the potential to provide all the necessary resources for its 2.7 million habitants. The current administrative structure prevents the optimum sharing of these resources.

ENERGY FLOW DIAGRAM

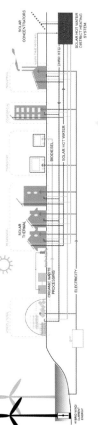

WATER FLOW DIAGRAM

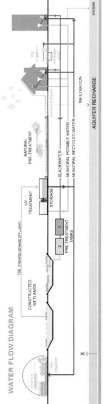

FIX A BLOCK
MALL CHOPPER
RE CENTER
RESI-DENSE
Densify residential fabric by inserting additional units around existing single family houses.

HICKSVILLE – A PILOT PROJECT

We have used Hicksville as test case. The LBC rules applied to all of Long Island can also be applied at this town scale. Although Hicksville has a street grid and block structure it is virtually spatially non-existent, since the majority of the downtown blocks are given over to surface parking for rail commuters. This lack of public space definition along with the absence of civic and commercial programs to generate activity makes for no sense of community. Rather than creating density by imposing an urban model of high rise apartment buildings we were looking for ways to achieve density while maintaining essential suburban qualities such as individuality, privacy, low-rise construction, and access to light, views, fresh air and nature.

5
Maintain essential suburban qualities by providing housing typologies with individual entrance door and private outdoor green space for each unit

6
Modify topography of new groundplane to optimize for solar access, views, cross ventilation, accessibility and parking capacity

4
Layer carpet of low-rise, high-density housing on new groundplane

3
Create new groundplane for new residential units

2
Provide covered, multi-story parking in the center of the block

1
Wrap blocks with a one story liner of public and retail program built to the lot line

EXISTING

semi-public and private outdoor spaces between houses

new groundplane dips down to sidewalk level for public access

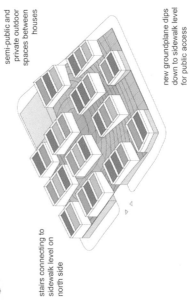

stairs connecting to sidewalk level on north side

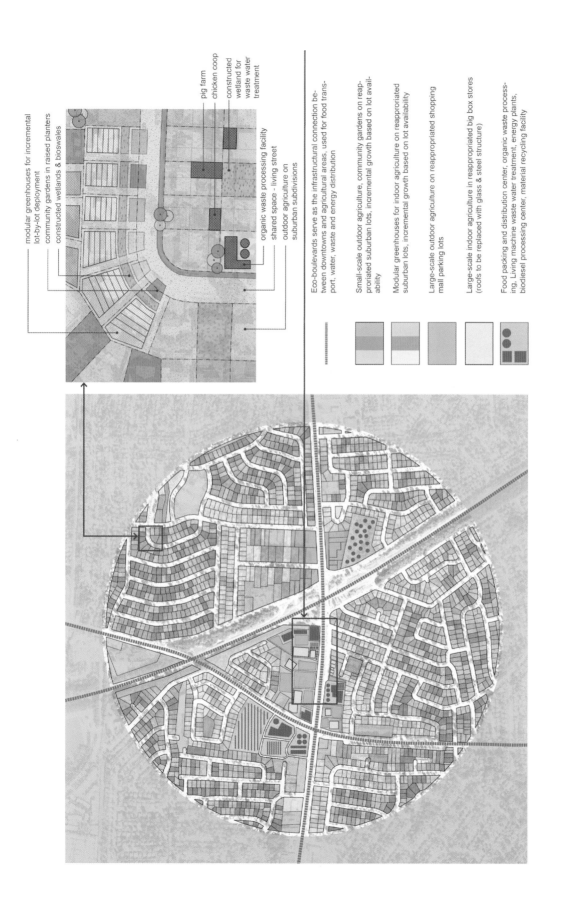

modular greenhouses for incremental lot-by-lot deployment

community gardens in raised planters

constructed wetlands & bioswales

pig farm

chicken coop

constructed wetland for waste water treatment

organic waste processing facility

shared space - living street

outdoor agriculture on suburban subdivisions

Eco-boulevards serve as the infrastructural connection between downtowns and agricultural areas, used for food transport, water, waste and energy distribution

Small-scale outdoor agriculture, community gardens on reappropriated suburban lots, incremental growth based on lot availability

Modular greenhouses for indoor agriculture on reappropriated suburban lots, incremental growth based on lot availability

Large-scale outdoor agriculture on reappropriated shopping mall parking lots

Large-scale indoor agriculture in reappropriated big box stores (roofs to be replaced with glass & steel structure)

Food packing and distribution center, organic waste processing, Living machine waste water treatment, energy plants, biodiesel processing center, material recycling facility

RE-CENTER

A new vibrant downtown plaza is centered around the train station, celebrating transit and creating an extension of the public space of the eco-boulevard thus connecting the train station and commuters to civic life, rather than cars.

RE-CENTER

A new vibrant downtown plaza is centered around the train station, celebrating transit and creating an extension of the public space of the eco-boulevard thus connecting the train station and commuters to civic life, rather than cars. The surrounding buildings have a slightly higher density and consist of more urban residential typologies that could be used as college dorms and assisted living.

FIX-A-BLOCK

The lack of public space definition and absence of civic and commercial programs to generate activity make for a lack of community life. Follow steps 1 - 6 on the right for how to fix downtown, one block at a time.

MALL CHOPPER

The same Fix A Block typological strategy would be applied to the large underutilized surface parking areas surrounding shopping malls which are subdivided into small blocks that echo the small grain of the surrounding context, resulting in a human scale that has long been lost.

100% LOCAL AGRICULTURE

Within the green belt is where 100% of Long Island's food will be grown. Modern, efficient agriculture practices will replenish nutrients into the ground, re-connect people with their food source, the land and its processes. Long island Radically Rezone becomes efficient yet abundant with beauty and opportunities for education and delight, thus arriving at a Living City.

The Living Market ___ Emily Talen and Sungduck Lee

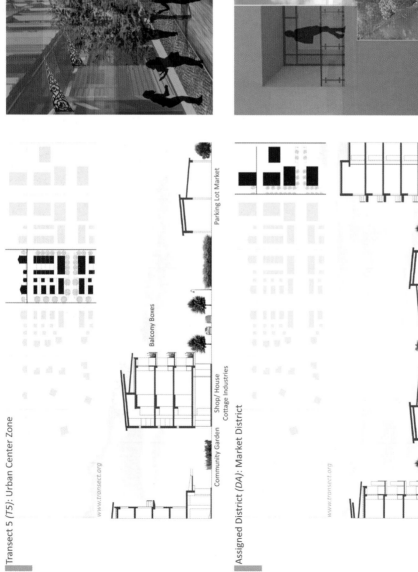

Transect 5 (T5): Urban Center Zone

www.transect.org

Community Garden   Shop/ House   Balcony Boxes   Parking Lot Market
                    Cottage Industries

Assigned District (DA): Market District

www.transect.org

Shop/ House   Parking Lot Market   Parking Lot Market   Parking Lot Market   Shop/ House
Food Markets   Cottage Industries

Themes
Supporting local economies, supporting social diversity, multiunit housing, suburban agriculture

Description
"The Living Market" proposal is about retrofitting suburban downtowns to support social diversity. The proposal envisions downtowns shared by affluent people and people on fixed incomes; people of varying racial, ethnic, and cultural backgrounds; teenagers and the elderly; married couples and singles; empty nesters and large families.

To connect a diverse community, we propose a centrally located, mixed-use marketplace as a common denominator that can act as a kind of community binder, with shop–house cottage industries and food markets, parking lot markets, and community gardens. "The Living Market" merges housing with small-scale markets. The proposal views the marketplace as a place where people work and live, rather than a tourist destination.

Reclaiming Community — Courtney Embrey and Michael Narciso

Themes

Ecological repair, transit-oriented development (TOD), supporting social diversity, suburban agriculture

Description

To reclaim is to save or recover something that has been affected by wrong doing or error and return it to its rightful course. The title of this project, "Reclaiming Community," refers to the goal of reclaiming two important communities within the Village of Hempstead: ecological and residential.

This proposal seeks to grow vertically instead of horizontally (promoting density over sprawl), maximize use of brownfield sites, establish educational programs, provide desirable affordable housing, and explore new ways of transit and mobility. In the process, it aims to restore the threatened Hempstead Plains habitat and provide a sustainable urban agricultural enterprise. These urban design strategies and programmatic elements can

generate a diverse demographic profile, enriching and providing opportunities for multigenerational and multicultural social interaction.

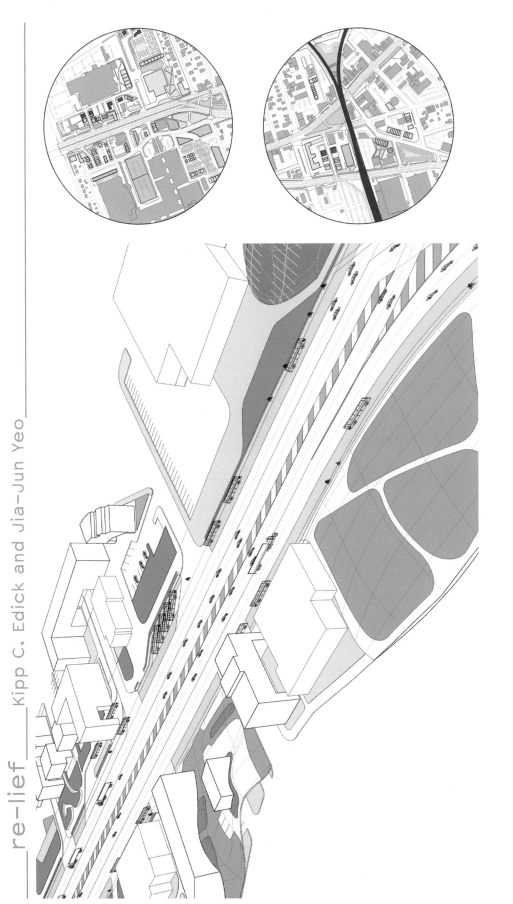

re-lief __Kipp C. Edick and Jia-Jun Yeo

Themes

Streetscape elements, retrofitting auto infrastructure, walkability, bottom-up tactics

Description

We saw the opportunity to rebuild Long Island literally from the ground up, with small-scale interventions. A typical Hicksville inhabitant, living in a place geared to the default use of the automobile, has to endure minutes of downtown traffic junctions in order to get a bottle of milk, a magazine, or visit the laundromat. Contrast this with downtown Manhattan, where all the needs of an apartment dweller are met within just a two-block radius.

We propose a new hardscape – of sidewalk, tree planters, newsstands, hard paving and even street lighting – that springs from bottom up, taking into account existing conditions and inhabitants. This new hardscape will enable a five- to ten-minute walk to the office, or a light jog to the deli, favoring neighborhoods that encourage human interaction and not traffic-light distraction.

The 21st Century Right-of-Way _Ian Caine and Derek Hoeferlin (co-lead designers), Jing Chen, Xi Chen, Akshita Sivakumar, and Jonathan Stitelman (team)

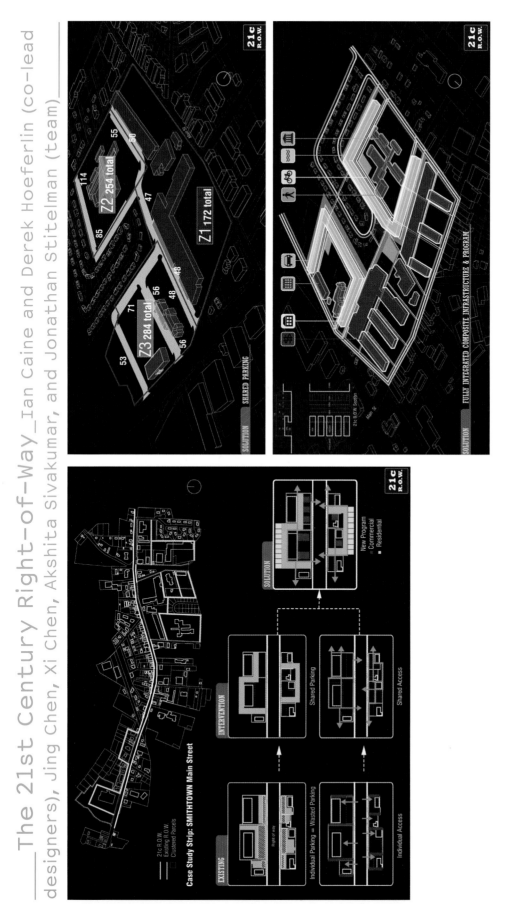

Themes

Transforming zoning, retrofitting auto infrastructure and shopping centers, infill development, walkability

Description

"21c R.O.W." is radical but real. It is a new suburban concept that will fundamentally alter the physical and legal structure of the strip. It is cost effective and ready for immediate implementation. We began with the assumption that we cannot "invent" a solution for our suburban predicament; we accept the prevalence of the automobile for the next 25 years while critiquing our reliance on uncoordinated, redundant parking infrastructure.

"21c R.O.W." requires collective thought and action. It is implemented locally through the introduction of a new, coordinated municipal zoning structure that balances public and private interests, by the addition of easements to support walkable infill when large parcels are subdivided. It repositions the public sector as the long term guardian of infrastructure and public space, while freeing up the private sector to do what it does best: innovate and money-make.

The Articulated Strip or, How the Strip Mall Can Save Suburbia

Judith K. De Jong and David Ruffing

1 STRIP
typical existing condition

2 FLIP
maintain density increased street setback

3 PROGRAM
insert uses to catalyze new relationships

4 STACK
determine type and density of housing

5 ARTICULATE
combine into new whole

the 24th/V Grind Café

RESIDENTIAL 4

RESIDENTIAL 1

PARKING

GROUND

2BR LOFT
1BR LOFT
CAR PATH
PEDESTRIAN PATH
PARKING
LIVE/WORK
RETAIL/CIVIC

Themes

Retrofitting shopping centers, innovative building types, infill development

Description

The strip mall has a remarkable systemized flexibility: it can accommodate many programs, be deployed many places, and produce many versions of its standard form. However, this potential has never been fully explored; rather, in its current guise, the strip mall typically produces islands of architectural and programmatic sameness, further isolated by seas of surface parking.

"The Articulated Strip" proposes a new, opportunistic strip typology that is highly adaptable to the specific conditions of its implementation, both programmatically and formally. The articulated strip can be deployed across medium or large sites, but is particularly effective at the scale of the suburban superblock, where its adaptability becomes most explicit. The strip mall and the superblock can be the generative agents of suburbia's re-formation.

Re:Define the Good Life_Sarah Hill

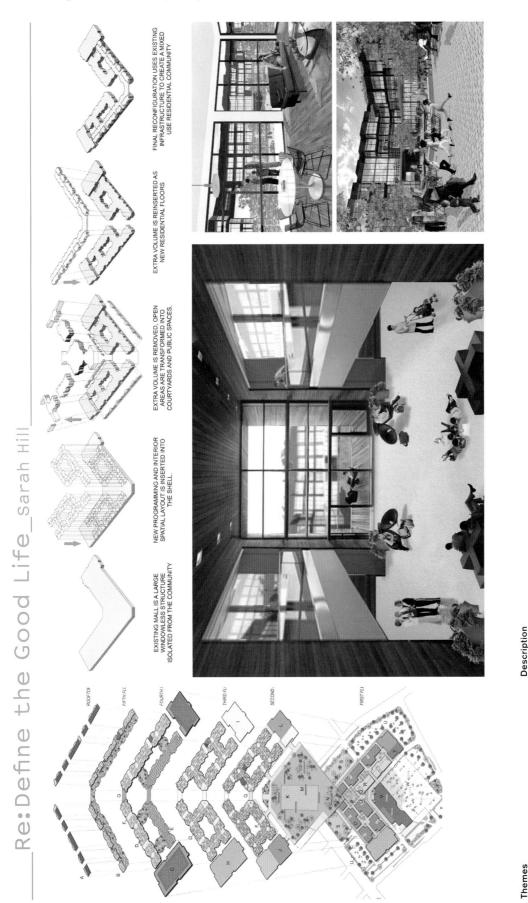

EXISTING MALL IS A LARGE WINDOWLESS STRUCTURE ISOLATED FROM THE COMMUNITY

NEW PROGRAMMING AND INTERIOR SPATIAL LAYOUT IS INSERTED INTO THE SHELL.

EXTRA VOLUME IS REMOVED, OPEN AREAS ARE TRANSFORMED INTO COURTYARDS AND PUBLIC SPACES.

EXTRA VOLUME IS REINSERTED AS NEW RESIDENTIAL FLOORS

FINAL RECONFIGURATION USES EXISTING INFRASTRUCTURE TO CREATE A MIXED USE RESIDENTIAL COMMUNITY

Description

Reimagined as a mixed-use micro community, a dead mall's existing infrastructure is reconnected to the existing town. Anchor stores are repurposed into a sporting complex. Parking lots are doubly efficient when used by shoppers in the day and by residents at night, with car share programs and bike storage.

Removal of superfluous interior square footage provides for a variety of outdoor public spaces, eliminating site isolation and heat island effect, while also allowing for residential backyards and rooftop community vegetable gardens. Economical modular housing components adjust to residential lifecycles, allowing residents to stay within the community longer and keep monthly expenses down. Modular components keep developers'

costs down. Rainwater and graywater reclamation reduce utility water usage and sewer overflow. Solar and wind energy production offsets demand from the power grid.

Themes

Retrofitting shopping centers, multiunit housing, modular building, adaptive reuse

REpark
Scalar Architecture (Julio Salcedo, Elizabeth MacWillie, and Jarman Acevedo)

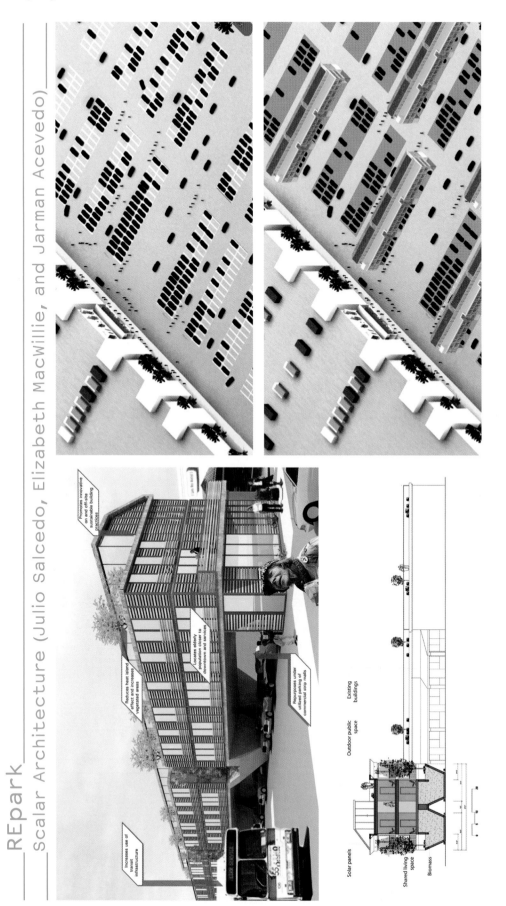

Increases use of transit infrastructure

Promotes innovative on and off-site sustainable building practices

Reduces heat island effect and increases vegetated areas

Locates elderly population closer to downtown and services

Repurposes under utilized parking of commercial strip malls

Solar panels

Outdoor public space

Existing buildings

Shared living space

Biomass

Themes

Housing choice for seniors, retrofitting shopping centers, innovative building types, new mass transit networks, modular building

Description

We identify a lightly built network of symbiotic uses in underutilized suburban commercial and retail parking lots. Within this light network we propose the addition of sustainable, flexible, modular units that sit lightly on the parking surface. The existing downtowns – left behind by the spatial and infrastructural demands of the late 20th century – are in turn inscribed into this emergent network by means of transit infrastructure: buses first, then light rail.

One scenario within our light network proposal validates our goals. It capitalizes on two factors that are essential aspects of Long Island: the current population of older adults and the emergent territories of under-utilized commercial strip malls. We call for the addition of modular assisted living facilities over selected parking lots of commercial malls, such as the Walt Whitman Mall at the intersection of 110 and the Jericho Turnpike.

Rail Park
Bergmann Associates (Michael Prattico, Tom Castelein, Jim Durfee, Mitch McAllister, and Shreya Shah)

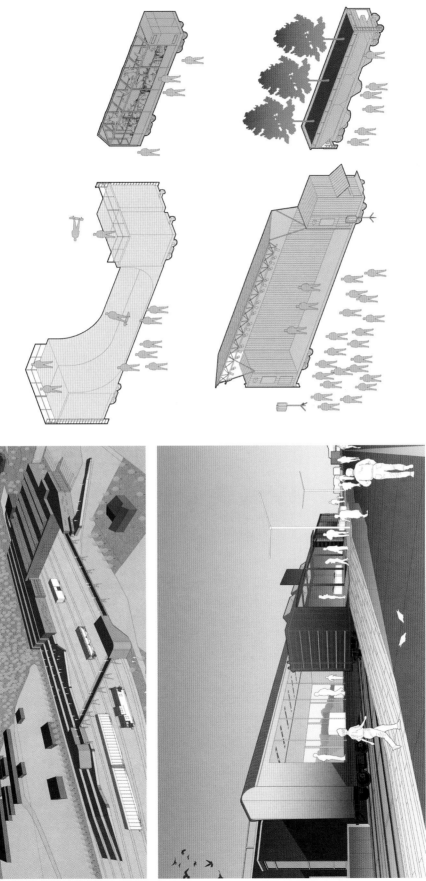

Themes
Cultural capital and the arts, transit-oriented development (TOD), landscape improvements, adaptive reuse

Description
Long Island downtowns owe their existence to the rail line. But the rail corridor is divisive and unattractive, and a boundary and impediment to the stimulus towns need to be lively and have a growing economy. Can interventions be made so that the rail space itself becomes a positive catalyst?

This proposal seeks to reclaim underutilized and disruptive track infrastructure, creating a linear activity armature that allows for recreation, art, and commerce in repurposed and re-imagined rail cars.

The new Rail Park corridor is animated by a rotating collection of repurposed rail cars. Passage along the corridor culminates at a former rail storage yard, converted to a center where the community can interact with artists and engineers who adapt rail equipment for use and display in the Rail Park or anywhere in the country.

Bethpage MoMA P.S. 2 _ Nelson Zhoujian Peng, Zhongwei Li, and Yang Wang_

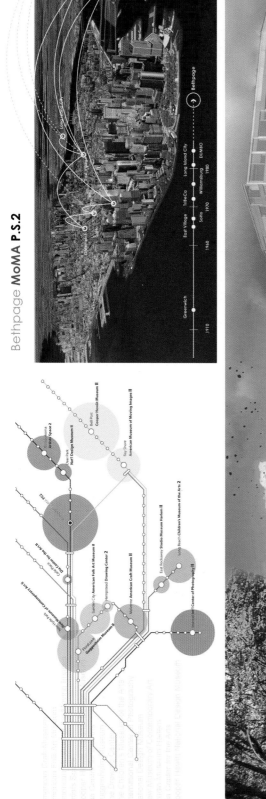

Bethpage **MoMA P.S.2**

Themes

Cultural capital and the arts, transit-oriented development (TOD), walkability, harnessing social networks

Description

Our design aims at channeling the influence of world-class art activities from Manhattan to centrally located Bethpage through the Long Island Rail Road system, establishing the second affiliated modern art institution for MoMA: MoMA P.S. 2.

In Bethpage, the spacious factories and warehouses of the industrial park area, walkable from the station, provide artists the space that expensive Manhattan is not able to provide; convenient transit offers frequent and easy connection with New York City. Artists would work here, live here, and socialize here, innovating the existing space, and fashioning a closely bounded community. This could feed into building a community that is less about the commute to New York City and is about truly living in the local. In Bethpage, TOD has evolved into Transit and Art Oriented Development (TAOD).

HIP Retrofit___David Kim, R. John Anderson, Seth Harry,
Padriac Steinschneider, Ela Dokonal, Mike Lydon, Will Dowdy, and Alex Latham III

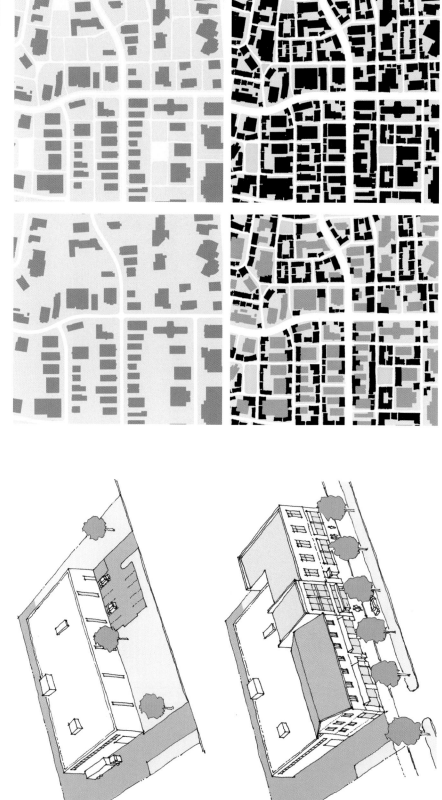

Themes

Retrofitting industrial parks, infill development, transit-oriented development (TOD), adaptive reuse, supporting local economies

Description

This project proposed a new north/south transit line through a place where 55,000 people already work, the Hauppauge Industrial Park (HIP). This 1,400 acre site is the largest industrial park in the Northeast U.S.

Big blocks and the big spaces between existing buildings present big opportunities for new infill projects. The HIP's large blocks can be divided

incrementally to introduce new streets and create building sites over time. There is enough space between the existing buildings to convert the current roadways into a network of boulevards with center through lanes separated from slip lanes by medians formed around the existing mature trees. Creating smaller blocks reveals that there is a great deal of space for higher density residential building types such

as row-houses, flats, lofts and live/work units and workplace "liner" buildings.

Enter\\Shift ___ Gordana Marjanovic

new - green

public space

public space

underground parking

Themes

Strengthening the public/civic realm, landscape improvements, infill development

Description

The project "Enter\Shift" is focused on revitalization of railway station areas as representative points of entry into the downtowns. The proposed principle of intervention is reorganization of parking lots (moving underground), leaving the ground free for people and public spaces, for establishing green structures that improve the environmental condition and provide people with necessary contact with nature and room for socialization.

The design itself is intended to be site specific, reflecting the identity of downtown Babylon, chosen because there is no public space around the station and sparse green can be found. The new space for Babylon Station is an entry point that tells a story about the suburb. Its wavy green structures and a water element symbolize the character of Babylon with its Argyle Lake, park and the coast. The first impression upon leaving the train is of proximity of these natural elements.

HuB–URB ___ Jing Su

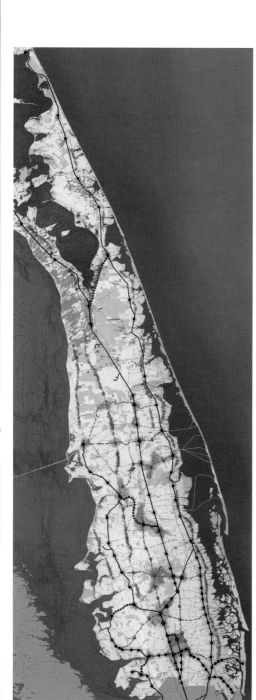

Themes

New mass transit networks, transit-oriented development (TOD), strengthening the public/civic realm, walkability

Description

This proposal looks closely at Long Island Rail Road stations and tries to transform them into true "hubs" for Long Island. At the regional level, a transit framework is conceptualized for Long Island that could use rail for intra–Long Island trips and moving goods, and to connect stations with a new and greener rapid transit system. Growth centers will be focused and restricted around transit hubs. Residences, workers, and visitors would be able to get to every necessary place by transit within Long Island. Suburban strip malls will lose their competitive edge to the mixed-use activities centers around transit hub. Their vast land could be used to restore natural resources.

With a regional guideline and action items at each station, Long Island could eventually reshape itself from "sub-urb" to "hub-urb."

LIFE Program ___ Edgar Papazian

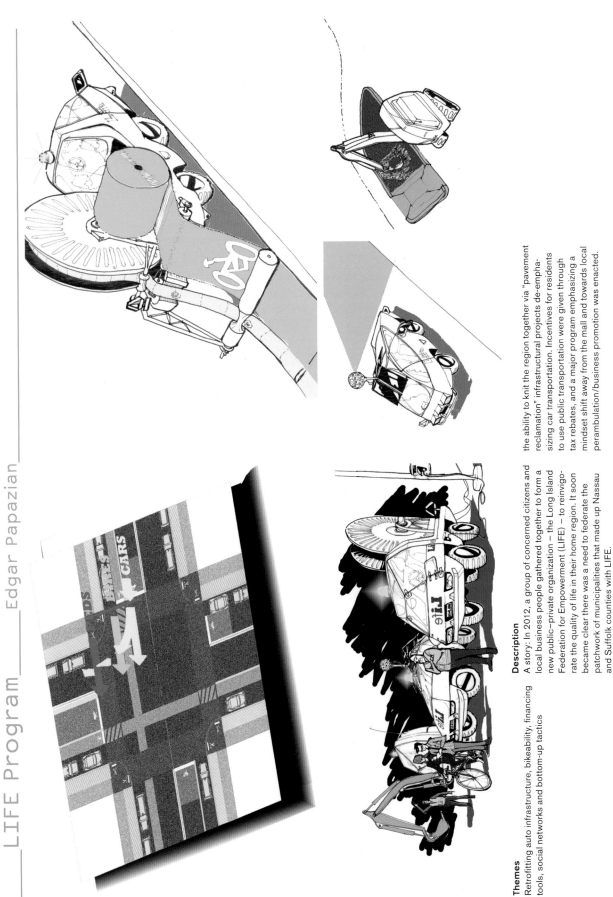

Themes
Retrofitting auto infrastructure, bikeability, financing tools, social networks and bottom-up tactics

Description
A story: In 2012, a group of concerned citizens and local business people gathered together to form a new public–private organization – the Long Island Federation for Empowerment (LIFE) – to reinvigorate the quality of life in their home region. It soon became clear there was a need to federate the patchwork of municipalities that made up Nassau and Suffolk counties with LIFE.

A major milestone was passed in 2014 when under the auspices of a new governor, LIFE was granted the ability to knit the region together via "pavement reclamation" infrastructural projects de-emphasizing car transportation. Incentives for residents to use public transportation were given through tax rebates, and a major program emphasizing a mindset shift away from the mall and towards local perambulation/business promotion was enacted.

The result: a walkable, bike-able, public transportation–rich sequence of communities, a jewel-like set of destinations.

Bike the Burb! — Hannah Hesse and Jochen Friedrichs

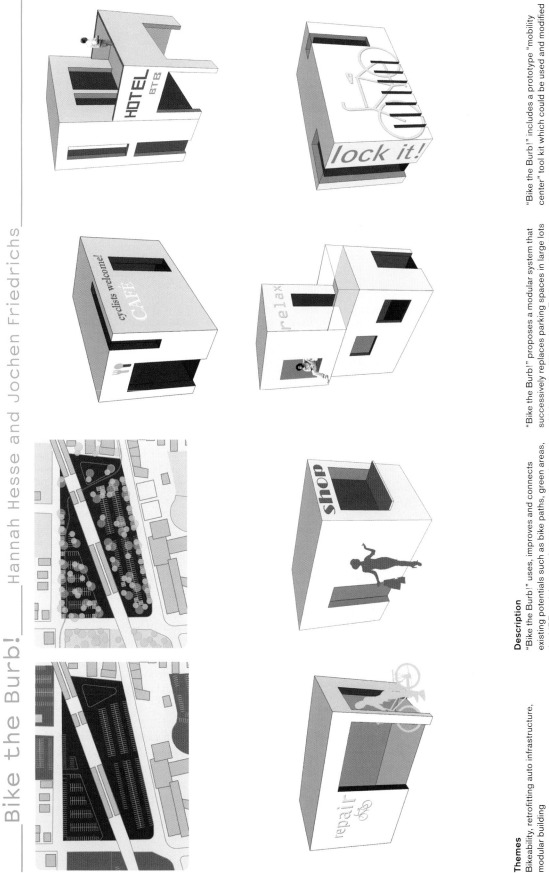

Themes

Bikeability, retrofitting auto infrastructure, modular building

Description

"Bike the Burb!" uses, improves and connects existing potentials such as bike paths, green areas, the LIRR and the waterfront to create a comfortable network of bike paths highly attractive for tourism (vacations, short trips, sports), residents (shopping, daily use, connecting people), and commuters (instead of using the car).

"Bike the Burb!" proposes a modular system that successively replaces parking spaces in large lots with boxes for different uses. Each motorist who becomes a cyclist makes space for one additional box, with exactly the dimensions of a car parking space. The proposal starts with a first mutated parking lot and will change step-by-step depending on need and interest of its users.

"Bike the Burb!" includes a prototype "mobility center" tool kit which could be used and modified in a participatory process by every Long Island suburb.

Conclusion

I present these visionary design proposals for better burbs to further productive discourse about the crucial role of design in global urbanization trends, human settlement patterns, urban morphology and form, and humankind's relationship and responsibilities to natural resources and a changing climate. The words *suburb* and *suburban* still carry potent meaning, hence the title of this book, *Designing Suburban Futures*. The topic has the potential to incite an astonishing level of sociopolitical vitriol and invective, seen blossoming in the blogosphere, even as it points directly to the deep identification and defensiveness, often on moral grounds, many feel about their personal settlement and lifestyle choices. These choices do matter, in the aggregate, as do the frameworks of policy, financing, infrastructure, development, and design that enable these choices to be made.

People who live in North American suburbs and consider themselves suburbanites know where they live. They know that they are not living in the city, although, depending on a multitude of factors, they may be less willing to acknowledge that their settlement context is, in a technical sense, urban. Likewise, those who live in center cities have difficulty conceding the same point, resisting recognition of the *urb* in *suburb*. The oppositional stance has made it difficult to tease out similarities and differences both between and within varied urbanized places. But tease we must.

Scholars and commentators, including me, debate the stakes of using the words *city* and *suburb* and implicating an enduring dichotomy and all that it has historically suggested about urban growth and form in regions with developed economies. As Build a Better Burb juror Allison Arieff reminds us, *suburb* may have "outlived its usefulness as a descriptive term – and as a model for future planning, at least in its current incarnation. Suburbs continue to be designed for homogeneity even though they're no longer homogeneous at all."

Similarly, we may be uncomfortable with connotations of the catchall phrase urban sprawl. We search for new terms to describe the complex geographies of urbanized metropolitan areas: *exurban*, *periurban*, *penurban*. I considered using other words, but it seemed crucial to preserve the legacies of the words *suburb* and *suburban* – both laudatory and pejorative – to help build the case that many aspects of suburban landscapes as we have known them in developed countries, particularly in the latter half of the twentieth century, are subject to dramatic change in this century. I propose in this book not only that change is inevitable but also that designers can, and must, play an active role in envisioning and shaping these future changes for better, more resilient suburban futures.

When the Build a Better Burb competition was first announced, many commentators from Long Island were skeptical about the impact of an ideas design competition, charging that the culture of resistance to change was too entrenched and that the visionary, imaginative nature of the design brief (the instructions to entrants) would produce schemes that would be incomprehensible to the general public and easily dismissed as irrelevant if not demonstrated to be immediately implementable. Contrary to expectations, the competition generated a great deal of interest and excitement, from both regional and national press, including an editorial in the *New York Times* titled "Blight Made Right" (May 17, 2010). The *Times* editors noted, "Good redevelopment ideas have died a million times on Long Island," while applauding the effort of the competition to plant optimism. "Somebody has to," they wrote, "and we're eager to see what grows."

Elected officials and other local leaders, with their fingers to the wind, are paying attention as the competition entries and the Build a Better Burb 2.0 website that the Long Island Index maintains introduce intriguing concepts that will, I am confident, have an impact on future redevelopment schemes and planning approaches on Long Island and elsewhere. The bar has been raised about what is deemed possible.

A note of caution is needed, however. When I questioned my fellow Build a Better Burb jurors in 2012 about the important fronts for suburban change right now, what strategies and tactics they advocate, whether there are optimal scales of intervention or time frames for transformation, their answers were revealing. Allison Arieff worries about political polarization and "the work the Tea Party is doing at planning commission meetings across the country, essentially by arguing for sprawl and advocating against any sustainable community efforts." She also warns against backlash to top-down visions, as presented in the Museum of Modern Art "Foreclosed" exhibit. Daniel D'Oca concurs that the political stakes of suburbia remain high, writing, "Historically, access to the suburbs meant access to good education, good jobs, good mortgages, low-crime neighborhoods, and even longer life expectancy. What matters most now is what has always mattered most: how do we increase minority and low-income populations' access to the suburbs and all of the 'goodies' that have historically accrued there?" He warns about accusations of elitism against planners who are overly critical of these "goodies," particularly when planning for people who are only now gaining access to them. Is it all to be taken away, just as they arrive?

Galina Tachieva, however, suggests that the pragmatics of economic opportunity will prevail over time to induce change and that immigrants and other new suburban arrivals will be drivers: "Suburbs have an overabundance of many things – infrastructure, national chains, big boxes, fast-food drive-throughs, lawns – but when suburbs start to fail, surplus becomes a liability. Reusing and adapting the existing suburban types to incubate new businesses will help catalyze the gradual completion of the rest of sprawl's incomplete fabric and make it more livable and sustainable in the long run." Architect Paul Lukez adds that

homeowners will become more proactive: "The increased cost of energy will over time require many to consider transforming the energy dependent systems (AC, heating, transport) that are so essential to suburban lifestyles. New modes of powering mobility will be considered, as will new more energy efficient heating and cooling systems. Some of these options may end up fostering new forms of community, centered on creating shared energy generating systems (solar, geo-tech)."

Robert Lane advocates expanded ideas about suburbs as productive landscapes. "Leo Marx's *The Machine in the Garden* is the definitive resource on the American way of thinking about the relationship between industry and the landscape – our schizophrenia embodied in the self-contradictory name of the 'industrial park' development type. Changes in manufacturing and the changing role of the suburbs as productive landscapes raise interesting questions about the place of industry in the suburbs and models for new kinds of mixed-use." At the U.S. Environmental Protection Agency, Lee S. Sobel is working to implement policies along these lines, seeking in particular to "mitigate the timing" issue in the development process with his notion of "Planned Retrofit."

All of these viewpoints – the need to confront political stalemate and hardening polemics against environmentally based arguments for change, advocacy for a community-based approach and cultural sensitivity to the desire for the traditional benefits of suburbia, recognition of opportunities to foment change when suburban "surpluses" and inefficiencies become liabilities, and exhortations to invent new suburban economic development paradigms that exploit and redirect established logics – are worth careful consideration. For the lives of many, there is much in the future at stake. Design has a potent and necessary role to play in the conversation.

Please, join in.

Epilogue:
New Roles
for Architecture
and Urban Design

To extend the conversation engendered by the Build a Better Burb competition and to place it in a larger historical, discursive, and advocacy context, I invited Kazys Varnelis into a reflective discussion via e-mail in the summer of 2012. In addition to being one of the competition's winning designers, Varnelis is the director of the Network Architecture Lab and a member of the architecture faculty at Columbia University. He is also a faculty member at the University of Limerick, Ireland. His books include *Blue Monday: Absurd Realities and Natural Histories* (2007), *Networked Ecologies in Los Angeles* (2008), *Networked Publics* (2008), and *The Philip Johnson Tapes: Interviews with Robert A. M. Stern* (2008).

From: JUNE WILLIAMSON

My goal in writing *Designing Suburban Futures* was to outline, for designers, planners, and policy-makers, myriad possibilities for helping to ensure future resiliency in suburbs. This resiliency can — and must — be pursued though proactive and productive engagement with design. To avoid doing so might prove disastrous to many regions, including New York's populous and waterlocked low-density suburbs on Long Island.

In developing the design brief for the Build a Better Burb (BBB) competition, we proposed that there had been a "crisis of imagination," and "bold new ideas" were urgently needed. I believe that many provocative, bold ideas were generated. The subsequent challenge for the sponsor, the Long Island Index, is to create social awareness and political will for translation of the design DNA of the most promising of these ideas into implementable proposals. The Long Island Index's director, Ann Golob, is focused on initiatives to use social media — the expanded and revised BBB website, professionally produced videos on Vimeo, exquisitely designed infographics, Twitter, and Facebook — to inform and engage people and to get productive conversations flowing.

Kazys, as a prolific scholar on networked publics and networked ecologies and as a suburbanite, what do you think of this strategy of focusing on social networking and online platforms rather than the more conventional route of direct engagement with local power elites?

From: KAZYS VARNELIS

Social networking and online platforms have to be part of almost any political engagement today. Avoiding them or thinking they are a fad would be like thinking newspapers, handbills, posters, and pamphlets were a fad in the eighteenth century.

That said, these are no magic bullets for reviving politics either. On the contrary, in *Networked Publics*, Merlyna Lim and Mark Kann observed that although networked media are great for mobilizing publics, they have thus far proved ineffective for promoting democratic deliberation.[1] That

essay, which they first drafted in 2006, has only been confirmed since then. On the eve of another presidential election, we seem further from a functioning civil society than ever. So sure, let's use social media to get the word out, but beyond that, I'm not sure we will get people in cities and suburbs talking to each other that easily via social media.

Now, as a competition, BBB is a form of deliberation. Individuals and groups make proposals, and then other individuals and groups deliberate about and vote on them. Could it be a model for other forms of deliberation?[2] I'd like to hear about your experience with this process. How well did it work?

From: JUNE WILLIAMSON

I absolutely agree that open ideas competitions are a form of deliberation, because of the involvement of expert juries and the complex process undertaken by sponsoring organizations — often nonprofits or public bodies — to assemble the brief. This is especially true when a larger public is invited to review and vote on submissions, as we did with BBB.[3] Ann Golob points to two significant impacts that resulted from the publicity around the competition: Long Islanders now generally accept the finding that there is a demographic brain drain such that the younger generation is leaving and that changes might be needed to attract them back, and that transit-served downtowns are important to the region's future.[4]

BBB itself was inspired by another competition, the ReBurbia call for ideas issued by *Dwell* magazine and Inhabitat.com in 2009. While developing our brief, I did comparative research into several other recent competitions, many also dealing with the suburban realm, such as Dead Malls (2003), Flip a Strip (2008), and TownShift (2010). We reached out to Galina Tachieva of the new urbanist firm DPZ, overwhelming winner of the People's Choice Award in ReBurbia for her "Urban Sprawl Repair Kit," to be a member of the jury. I think she won with the public because her before-and-after axonometric illustrations are so clear and imageable.

Design competitions are perhaps a particularly fertile form of deliberation, a delightful device to solicit, introduce, and circulate imaginative propositions in ways not permitted or enabled by other deliberative forums. I feel strongly that more suburban communities should consider engaging youthful design talent and energy with competitions or similar proactive initiatives.

The challenge then becomes how to pursue implementation. One response to this challenge is the movement advocating tactical urbanism and spontaneous interventions, the topic of the U.S. Pavilion at the 2012 International Venice Architecture Biennale. The turn to short-term, do-it-yourself actions reflects frustration with the slow pace of change and the drying up of official channels for funding and support. Another response is to call for more robust insertions of design thinking into national, state, and metropolitan policy discussions, recognizing the upstream sources from which much funding flows.

What do you think of top-down versus bottom-up solutions to regional challenges? What about short-term versus long-term horizons for change? How much time have we got?

From: KAZYS VARNELIS

Not enough!

The political stalemate around us needs to be broken, and it needs to be broken fast. That said, I wish I could be optimistic, but it's hard to be. There are massive problems in our society today that are making governance increasingly difficult.

Governance is broken at many local levels. In *American Metropolitics: The New Suburban Reality*, Myron Orfield looks at how this crazy quilt of local governments produces barriers to effective governance.[5] Some suburbs (and cities, such as New York) do very well, others do not. But the haves don't want to fund the have-nots. As a country, we need to start thinking about creating broader regional initiatives. Rebuilding suburbs involves rebuilding the political structures that are involved.

But it's not easy to do. This is something we tried to do with our "Long Division" project. We concluded that Long Island would face socioeconomic and environmental crises over the next half century, over freshwater scarcity and persistent

racial and socioeconomic inequity, if regional governments capable of taking unprecedented action didn't form. It would make tremendous sense to concentrate growth in the western end, better served with infrastructure, and let the eastern end shrink, preventing development and turning empty space into parkland and nature preserve, an amenity for everyone that would allow much greater water infiltration into the aquifer.

Now we didn't expect we'd win the People's Choice Award for this project. It's obviously going to be controversial. However, we were hoping to introduce an issue for discussion. Still, people are going to be hurt by this. Nobody wants to see his or her town or neighborhood go away. Everyone wants to get rich from real estate; nobody wants to see it become worthless. But these are the kind of issues that not only Long Island but communities across the country need to confront.

Moreover, we need to do this fast. Many of the changes I am talking about are long term but require us to act swiftly to get under way. We are facing big challenges. This isn't to say that short-term projects aren't useful. They are. But we've been putting off the inevitable for too long. Crisis is at hand across the country, and we saw the first wave crest in the aftermath of 2008. Things aren't going to get better soon.

From: JUNE WILLIAMSON

So where do we sit with design competitions? I think they can play a vital role in the process of mediating between top-down and bottom-up realms. Much analysis of metropolitan management and growth challenges points to jurisdictional boundaries as a source of barriers to implementation of new, ecologically informed systems thinking for urban infrastructure, such as is needed for managing freshwater, regardless of which political party is in power. These boundaries range from the scale of lot lines to municipal borders, tangled layerings and misalignments of water, fire, transportation, and school districts, and even state borders that dissect metropolitan areas, such as New York, New Jersey, and Connecticut.

Orfield's work is an apt reference. Restructuring governance is at root about designing frameworks that move us beyond city versus suburb and suburb versus suburb divides, to permit sharper focus on redressing gross social and economic inequalities and sharing stewardship of ecological resources.

In the introduction to this book I emphasized two simple points. First, it may be that the greatest gains in overall resiliency are to be made in suburbs. Second, close study of the history, present, and future potential of the suburban form in already hyperurbanized regions, such as North America, offers valuable cautionary tales and illuminating lessons for currently urbanizing places across the globe.

Are suburbs really that important to future urban resiliency? Does suburban history matter, in global terms?

From: KAZYS VARNELIS

Yes, suburbs are still crucial. There's been a lot in the press about how more people live in urban areas than in any other form of habitation today, about how cities have grown so much in the last two decades, about the revival of cities and so on, about hyperdensity, but much of that talk is naive. Let's take these point by point. First, when geographers speak of urban or metropolitan areas, they include suburbs. What's the only completely urbanized state in the union according to the Census Bureau? New Jersey. Now it's true that more than 85 percent of the U.S. population lives in metropolitan areas, but it may be more useful to say that more than 50 percent of the U.S. population now lives in suburban areas. How about China, that land of hyperdensity? Well, suburbanization is getting going there too, and all that fabulous high-speed rail is going to give distant suburbs a big boost.[6] As for the revival of cities in this country, few older cites have grown recently, and the growth of urban centers in the last decade has slowed down in comparison to the 1990s urban renaissance.[7] Manhattan, to take the most vaunted example, is still far below its peak in population a century ago.[8] Some center cities, such as Detroit, are doing very badly, and a huge number, particularly those that resemble traditional cities, are struggling. Other cities, such as Las Vegas, Phoenix, and Tucson, resemble suburbs much more than cities.

And then there's the social justice issue. Why is it that the poor, particularly poor African Americans, are moving out of New York, Chicago, and Los Angeles? It's not so appropriate to be smug about the reversal of white flight when blacks are leaving. Moreover, when they aren't moving to generally suburban environments in the New South, poor blacks — and other disadvantaged people — are moving to the suburbs where life is cheaper and sometimes better than in their old communities. Inner-ring suburbs are densifying and becoming much more diverse, if not outrightly dominated by minorities. We could be seeing the dawn of a new kind of segregation, convenient for urban and suburban NIMBYists alike. Nor is this different elsewhere.

Suburbs and city cores developed at the same time in the United States. You're not going to have a dense urban core without the commuters into the city or the vast number of business networks in the suburban metropolitan areas, not in this country and not in most countries. Suburban past, present, and future are key to any understanding of the city. You can't peel these two geographies apart.

From: JUNE WILLIAMSON

I agree. Metropolitan geographies are increasingly diverse and complex, and to think only of "cities" when considering global urbanization is to miss the point. What are the main fronts for change in architectural and urban design discourse? Where do we go from here?

From: KAZYS VARNELIS

Defying any logic, architecture discourse continues to be overly tied to form. Surely we aren't a postmodern culture anymore — after all, it's been 35, if not 40, years since modernism gave way to postmodernism. So why this postmodern overemphasis on form? Architects may still be intoxicated by the heady days of the building boom, but we need to recognize that the issues we face are bigger and are either threats to our future or opportunities, depending on how we view them. The transformations in relationships of city and suburb that we have been discussing here are among the most critical of fronts in architecture as they address the sustainability of both form of habitation as well as issues of social justice. The suburb isn't going away, and neither is the ongoing tension between it and the city. Architects of all stripes need to tackle these questions or risk increasing irrelevance at an urban level.

Notes

1. Kazys Varnelis, ed., *Networked Publics* (Cambridge, MA: MIT Press, 2008).

2. The Wolfson Prize, for example, offers £250,000 for proposals to break up the Euro in an orderly fashion.

3. We received constructive feedback — also a form of deliberation — that two dozen finalists were too many projects to process and evaluate on a website, no matter how well designed.

4. Interview of Ann Golob by author, June 7, 2012.

5. Myron Orfield, *American Metropolitics: The New Suburban Reality* (Washington, DC: Brookings Institution Press, 2002).

6. Bill Powell, "The Short March," *Time* (February 14, 2008), http://www.time.com/time/magazine/article/0,9171,1713336-1,00.html.

7. Haya El Nasser, "Suburban Growth Focused on Inner and Outer Communities," *USA Today* (May 5, 2011), http://www.usatoday.com/news/nation/2011-04-26-suburbs-growth-census-demographics_n.htm.

8. Amy O'Leary, "Everybody Inhale. How Many People Can Manhattan Hold?" *New York Times* (March 1, 2012), http://www.nytimes.com/2012/03/04/realestate/how-many-people-can-manhattan-hold.html.

Selected Bibliography

Classics on the History of Suburbia

Fishman, Robert. 1987. *Bourgeois Utopias: The Rise and Fall of Suburbia*. New York: Basic Books.

Hayden, Dolores. 2003. *Building Suburbia: Green Fields and Urban Growth, 1820–2000*. New York: Pantheon.

Jackson, Kenneth T. 1985. *Crabgrass Frontier: The Suburbanization of the United States*. New York: Oxford University Press.

Kruse, Kevin M., and Thomas J. Sugrue. 2006. *The New Suburban History*. Chicago: University of Chicago Press.

Nicolaides, Becky M., and Andrew Wiese, eds. 2006. *The Suburb Reader*. New York: Routledge.

Books on Suburbia and Suburban and Urban Design Issues

Angel, S., J. Parent, D. L. Civco, and A. M. Blei. 2012. *Atlas of Urban Expansion*. Cambridge, MA: Lincoln Institute of Land Policy.

Barnett, Jonathan. 2003. *Redesigning Cities: Principles, Practice, Implementation*. Chicago: APA Planners Press.

Ben-Joseph, Eran. 2012. *ReThinking a Lot: The Design and Culture of Parking*. Cambridge, MA: MIT Press.

Bergdoll, Barry, and Reinhold Martin. 2012. *Foreclosed: Rehousing the American Dream*. New York: Museum of Modern Art.

Blauvelt, Andrew, ed. 2008. *Worlds Away: New Suburban Landscapes*. Minneapolis: Walker Art Center.

Bohl, Charles C. 2002. *Place Making: Developing Town Centers, Main Streets, and Urban Villages*. Washington, DC: Urban Land Institute.

Campoli, Julie, and Alex S. MacLean. 2007. *Visualizing Density*. Cambridge, MA: Lincoln Institute of Land Policy. Online resources at http://www.lincolninst.edu/subcenters/visualizing-density/.

Chase, John, Margaret Crawford, and John Kaliski. 2008. *Everyday Urbanism*, updated and expanded. New York: Monacelli.

Childs, Mark C. 2012. *Urban Composition: Developing Community through Design*. New York: Princeton Architectural Press.

Chow, Renee. 2002. *Suburban Space: The Fabric of Dwelling*. Berkeley: University of California Press.

Christensen, Julia. 2008. *Big Box Reuse*. Cambridge, MA: MIT Press.

Cisneros, Henry, Margaret Dyer-Chamberlain, and Jane Hickie, eds. 2012. *Independent for Life: Homes and Neighborhoods for an Aging America*. Austin: University of Texas Press.

Condon, Patrick M. 2010. *Seven Rules for Sustainable Communities: Design Strategies for the Post-Carbon World*. Washington, DC: Island Press.

Davis, Howard. 2012. *Living over the Store: Architecture and Local Urban Life*. New York: Routledge.

Duany, Andrés, Elizabeth Plater-Zyberk, and Jeff Speck. 2000. *Suburban Nation: The Rise of Sprawl and the Decline of the American Dream*. New York: North Point Press.

Dunham-Jones, Ellen, and June Williamson. 2011. *Retrofitting Suburbia: Urban Design Solutions for Redesigning Suburbs*, updated edition. Hoboken, NJ: Wiley.

Dunster, Bill, Craig Simmons, and Bobby Gilbert. 2008. *The ZEDbook: Solutions for a Shrinking World*. London: Taylor & Francis.

Ewing, Reid, Keith Bartholomew, Steve Winckelman, Jerry Walters, and Don Chen, with Barbara McCann and David Goldberg. 2008. *Growing Cooler: The Evidence on Urban Development and Climate Change.* Washington, DC: Urban Land Institute.

Farr, Douglas. 2008. *Sustainable Urbanism: Urban Design with Nature.* Hoboken, NJ: Wiley.

Florida, Richard. 2010. *The Great Reset: How the Post-Crash Economy Will Change the Way We Live and Work.* New York: Harper.

Frumkin, Howard, Lawrence Frank, and Richard Jackson. 2004. *Urban Sprawl and Public Health: Designing, Planning, and Building for Healthy Communities.* Washington, DC: Island Press.

Garreau, Joel. 1991. *Edge City: Life on the New Frontier.* New York: Doubleday.

Girling, Cynthia, and Ronald Kellett. 2005. *Skinny Streets and Green Neighborhoods: Design for Environment and Community.* Washington, DC: Island Press.

Haeg, Fritz, Will Allen, and Diana Balmori. 2010. *Edible Estates: Attack on the Front Lawn*, 2nd revised edition. New York: Metropolis Books.

Hanlon, Bernadette, John Rennie Short, and Thomas J. Vicino. 2010. *Cities and Suburbs: New Metropolitan Realities in the US.* New York: Routledge.

Hayden, Dolores, with Jim Wark. 2004. *A Field Guide to Sprawl.* New York: Norton.

Heinberg, Richard, and Daniel Lerch, eds. 2010. *The Post Carbon Reader: Managing the 21st Century's Sustainability Crises.* Healdsburg, CA: Watershed Media.

Jacobs, Allan B., Elizabeth Macdonald, and Yodan Rofé. 2002. *The Boulevard Book: History, Evolution, Design of Multiway Boulevards.* Cambridge, MA: MIT Press.

Kelbaugh, Doug, ed. 1989. *The Pedestrian Pocket Book: A New Suburban Design Strategy.* New York: Princeton Architectural Press.

Kelbaugh, Douglas, and Kit Krankel McCullough, eds. 2008. *Writing Urbanism.* New York: Routledge.

Leinberger, Christopher B. 2007. *The Option of Urbanism: Investing in a New American Dream.* Washington, DC: Island Press.

Loukaitou-Sideris, Anastasia, and Renia Ehrenfeucht. 2009. *Sidewalks: Conflict and Negotiation over Public Space.* Cambridge, MA: MIT Press.

Lukez, Paul. 2007. *Suburban Transformations.* New York: Princeton Architectural Press.

Lynch, Kevin. 1960. *The Image of the City.* Cambridge, MA: MIT Press.

Marx, Leo. 1964. *The Machine in the Garden: Technology and the Pastoral Ideal in America.* Oxford, England: Oxford University Press.

Nelson, Arthur C. 2013. *Reshaping Metropolitan America: Development Trends and Opportunities to 2030.* Washington, DC: Island Press.

Newman, Peter, Timothy Beatley, and Heather Boyer. 2009. *Resilient Cities: Responding to Peak Oil and Climate Change.* Washington, DC: Island Press.

Niedt, Christopher W., ed. 2013. *Social Justice in Diverse Suburbs: History, Politics, and Prospects.* Philadelphia: Temple University Press.

Oldenburg, Ray. 1997. *The Great Good Place: Cafés, Coffee Shops, Community Centers, Beauty Parlors, General Stores, Bars, Hangouts, and How They Get You through the Day.* New York: Marlowe.

Orfield, Myron. 2002. *American Metropolitics: The New Suburban Reality.* Washington, DC: Brookings Institution Press.

Owens, Bill. 1973. *Suburbia.* San Francisco: Straight Arrow Books.

Rome, Adam. 2001. *The Bulldozer in the Countryside: Suburban Sprawl and the Rise of American Environmentalism.* New York: Cambridge University Press.

Rowe, Peter. 1991. *Making a Middle Landscape.* Cambridge, MA: MIT Press.

Saunders, William, ed. 2005. *Sprawl and Suburbia: A Harvard Design Magazine Reader.* Minneapolis: University of Minnesota Press.

Scheer, Brenda Case. 2010. *The Evolution of Urban Form: Typology for Planners and Architects.* Chicago: American Planning Association.

Sobel, Lee S., with Ellen Greenberg and Steven Bodzin. 2002. *Greyfields into Goldfields: Dead Malls Become Living Neighborhoods.* San Francisco: Congress for the New Urbanism.

Sorkin, Michael, ed. 1992. *Variations on a Theme Park: The New American City and the End of Public Space.* New York: The Noonday Press.

Stanilov, Kiril, and Brenda Case Scheer, eds. 2004. *Suburban Form: An International Perspective.* New York: Routledge.

Stein, Clarence S. 1957. *Toward New Towns for America.* Cambridge, MA: MIT Press.

Stern, Robert A. M., and John Massengale. 1981. *The Anglo-American Suburb: AD Profile.* London: Architectural Design.

Tachieva, Galina. 2010. *Sprawl Repair Manual.* Washington, DC: Island Press.

Talen, Emily. 2008. *Design for Diversity: Exploring Socially Mixed Neighbourhoods.* London: Architectural Press.

Venturi, Robert, Denise Scott Brown, and Steven Izenour. 1977. *Learning from Las Vegas*, revised edition. Cambridge, MA: MIT Press.

Reports, Book Chapters, and Articles in Print or Online

Angel, Shlomo, with Jason Parent, Daniel L. Civco, and Alejandro M. Blei. 2010. *The Persistent Decline in Urban Densities: Global and Historical Evidence of "Sprawl."* Cambridge, MA: Lincoln Institute of Land Policy Working Paper (July).

Arieff, Allison. 2012. "Opinionator" blog for the *New York Times.* http://opinionator.blogs.nytimes.com/category/allison-arieff/.

Armborst, Tobias, Daniel D'Oca, and Georgeen Theodore. 2009. Community: The American way of living. *Places* online. http://places.designobserver.com/entry.html?entry=10647.

Bohl, Charles C., with Elizabeth Plater-Zyberk. 2006. Building community across the rural-to-urban transect. *Places* 18:1(Spring):4–17. http://escholarship.org/uc/item/1zt6g0sr.

Brill, Michael. 2001. Problems with mistaking community life for public life. *Places* 14(2):48–55. http://escholarship.org/uc/item/5d67x283.

Center for Transit-Oriented Development. *Hidden in Plain Sight: Capturing the Demand for Housing Near Transit*. Oakland, CA: Reconnecting America, September 2004, revised April 2005. http://www.reconnectingamerica.org/public/reports.

Dunham-Jones, Ellen, and June Williamson, guest editors. 2005. Retrofitting suburbia. *Places* 17:2 (Summer). http://escholarship.org/uc/ced_places?volume=17;issue=2.

Dunham-Jones, Ellen, and June Williamson. 2008. Instant cities, instant architecture, and incremental metropolitanism. *Harvard Design Magazine* 28, online (Spring/Summer). http://www.gsd.harvard.edu/research /publications/hdm/back/28_DunhamJonesWilliamson.html.

Dunham-Jones, Ellen, and June Williamson. 2009. Retrofitting suburbia. *Urban Land* 68:6(June):38–47. http://www.uli.org/.../Magazines /UrbanLand/.../UrbanLand/.../Jones.ashx.

Elliott, Donald. 2010. *Premature Subdivisions and What to Do about Them*. Lincoln Institute of Land Policy working paper. http://www.lincolninst.edu/pubs/1761_Premature-Subdivisions-and-What-to-Do-About-Them.

Ellis, Erle C., Kees Klein Goldewijk, Stefan Siebert, Deborah Lightman, and Navin Ramankutty. 2010. Anthropogenic transformation of the biomes, 1700 to 2000. *Global Ecology and Biogeography* 19:5(September):589–606. http://ecotope.org/anthromes/paradigm/.

Hayden, Dolores. 1981. What would a non-sexist city be like? Speculations on housing, urban design, and human work. In *Women and the American City*, edited by Catharine R. Stimpson et al., 49–57. Chicago: University of Chicago Press.

Institute of Transportation Engineers and the Congress for the New Urbanism. 2010. *Designing Walkable Urban Thoroughfares: A Context Sensitive Approach: An ITE Recommended Practice*. http://www.ite.org/css/.

Mehaffy, Michael, Sergio Porta, et al. 2010. Urban nuclei and the geometry of streets: The "emergent neighborhoods" model. *Urban Design International* 15:22–46.

Nelson, Arthur C. 2006. Leadership in a new era. *Journal of the American Planning Association* 72:4(Autumn):393–407.

Payton, Neal, and Brian O'Looney. 2006. Seeking urbane parking solutions. *Places* 18:1(Spring). http://escholarship.org/uc/item/0897x236.

Scheer, Brenda Case. 2001. The anatomy of sprawl. *Places* 14:2. http://escholarship.org/uc/item/4mt5561r.

Southworth, Michael. 2005. Reinventing Main Street: From mall to townscape mall. *Journal of Urban Design* 10:2(June):151–70.

Street Plans Collaborative, Mike Lydon, ed. 2012. *Tactical Urbanism Handbook*, 2. http://issuu.com/streetplanscollaborative/docs /tactical_urbanism_vol_2_final.

Online Resources

American Institute of Architects Sustainable Design Assessment Team program: http://www.aia.org/about/initiatives/AIAS075425

Atlanta Regional Commission's Livable Centers Initiative: http://www.atlantaregional.com/html/308.aspx

Brookings Institution Metropolitan Policy Program: http://www.brookings.edu/METRO.ASPX

Build a Better Burb, a project of the Long Island Index, sponsored by the Rauch Foundation: http://buildabetterburb.org/; http://www.longislandindex.org/

Center for Neighborhood Technology, Housing + Transportation Index: http://htaindex.cnt.org/

Congress for the New Urbanism, Sprawl Retrofit Initiative: http://www.cnu.org/sprawlretrofit

Cultures of the Suburbs International Research Network: http://suburbs.exeter.ac.uk/

Lincoln Institute of Land Policy: http://www.lincolninst.edu/

Making Room, sponsored by Citizens Housing and Planning Council and the Architectural League of New York: http://makingroomnyc.com

National Resources Defense Council, "Smart Growth" issue page: http://www.nrdc.org/smartgrowth/default.asp

National Trust for Historic Preservation "Main Street" Center: http://www.preservationnation.org/main-street/

Project for Public Spaces: http://www.pps.org/

Reconnecting America: http://www.reconnectingamerica.org/

Regional Plan Association of New York, New Jersey and Connecticut, program on community design: http://www.rpa.org/community_design.html

Spontaneous Interventions: Design Actions for the Common Good, U.S. Pavilion 2012 Venice Architecture Biennale: http://www.spontaneousinterventions.org

Streetsblog: http://www.streetsblog.org/

U.S. Green Building Council's LEED for Neighborhood Development: http://www.usgbc.org/DisplayPage.aspx?CMSPageID=148

World Urbanization Prospects, United Nations, Department of Economic and Social Affairs, Population Division: http://esa.un.org/unpd/wup/index.html

Credits

Pages xviii–xxi: *Ciphers*, © Christoph Gielen.

Page 4: Alexander Jackson Davis Architectural Drawings Collection, PR016 #564 and #565. Collection of The New-York Historical Society.

Page 5, left: National Gallery of Art, Washington, DC, USA. Gift of Mrs. Huddleston Rogers.

Page 5, right: Courtesy of the Riverside Historical Museum.

Page 6: Courtesy of Angela Strassheim.

Page 7, right: Photo courtesy of Stephen L. Meyers.

Page 8, left: From the Collections of The Henry Ford.

Page 8, right: Agroventures, Graeme Murray Filtered Vision, 2012.

Page 9, left: First Garden City Heritage Museum, http://www.gardencitymuseum.org.

Page 9, right: Diagram from Clarence S. Stein, *Toward New Towns for America*, 1957, 42.

Page 10: Photo by Thomas Faust, 2012.

Page 11: Photo by Skot Weidemann. Frank Lloyd Wright Foundation, Scottsdale, AZ / Artists Rights Society (ARS), NY.

Page 12: Photograph courtesy of James Ewing. © 2011 James Ewing. Image courtesy of WORKac.

Page 13: Library of Congress, Prints & Photographs Division, FSA/OWI Collection, LC-USF34-063658-D and LC-USF34-063681-D.

Page 14: Library of Congress, Prints & Photographs Division, FSA/OWI Collection, LC-USF34-063747-D and LC-USF34-063679-D.

Page 15: Federal Home Loan Bank Board, Records of the City Survey Program, RG 195, 450/68/03/02, National Archives II, College Park, MD.

Page 16: © Bill Owens Archives.

Page 17, left: Library of Congress, Prints & Photographs Division, LC-USZ62-132141.

Page 17, right: © Estate of William A. Garnett. Courtesy of J. Paul Getty Museum, Los Angeles.

Page 18: © Bill Owens Archives.

Page19: Photo by Lee Quill, AIA, 2011.

Page 20: © Martin Parr/Magnum Photos.

Page 23: Matthew Niederhauser/INSTITUTE.

Page 25: Photo by Tom Bernard. Courtesy of Venturi, Scott Brown and Associates, Inc.

Page 26, left: Courtesy of Duany Plater-Zyberk & Company, Architects and Town Planners.

Page 26, right: Courtesy of Alexander Gorlin Architects.

Page 27, left: Courtesy of Calthorpe Associates.

Page 27, right: © OMA.

Page 28: Courtesy of Michael Sorkin Studio.

Page 29: Urban Advantage.

Page 30: Courtesy of Interboro Partners.

Page 31: © Paul Lukez Architecture, 2007.

Page 32, left: Courtesy of Galina Tachieva and Duany Plater-Zyberk & Company, Architects and Town Planners, 2010.

Page 32, right: Courtesy of June Williamson and Anne Vaterlaus.

Page 36: © Gregory Crewdson. Courtesy Gagosian Gallery.

Page 53: Long Island Index.

Page 54: Long Island Index Interactive Map and Bing.

Pages 59, 60: Photos by Kelly Greenfield, 2010.

Page 61: Long Island Index.

Index

About Island Press

Since 1984, the nonprofit Island Press has been stimulating, shaping, and communicating the ideas that are
essential for solving environmental problems worldwide.
With more than 800 titles in print and some 40 new
releases each year, we are the nation's leading publisher
on environmental issues. We identify innovative thinkers
and emerging trends in the environmental field. We work
with world-renowned experts and authors to develop cross-
disciplinary solutions to environmental challenges.

Island Press designs and implements coordinated book
publication campaigns in order to communicate our critical
messages in print, in person, and online using the latest
technologies, programs, and the media. Our goal: to reach
targeted audiences – scientists, policymakers, environmental advocates, the media, and concerned citizens – who
can and will take action to protect the plants and animals
that enrich our world, the ecosystems we need to survive,
the water we drink, and the air we breathe.

Island Press gratefully acknowledges the support of
its work by the Agua Fund, Inc., The Margaret A. Cargill
Foundation, Betsy and Jesse Fink Foundation, The William
and Flora Hewlett Foundation, The Kresge Foundation,
The Forrest and Frances Lattner Foundation, The Andrew
W. Mellon Foundation, The Curtis and Edith Munson
Foundation, The Overbrook Foundation, The David and
Lucile Packard Foundation, The Summit Foundation, Trust
for Architectural Easements, The Winslow Foundation, and
other generous donors.

The opinions expressed in this book are those of
the author(s) and do not necessarily reflect the views
of our donors.

Island Press Board of Directors